# FAITH IN

Also by George Guiver CR and published by SPCK:

*Company of Voices* (1988)

George Guiver CR

# *Faith in Momentum*

## THE DISTINCTIVENESS OF THE CHURCH

First published in Great Britain 1990
SPCK
Holy Trinity Church
Marylebone Road
London NW1 4DU

Thanks are due to the following for permission to reproduce
copyright material:

Duckworth, London, and University of Notre Dame Press, Indiana,
for the extract from *After Virtue* by Alasdair MacIntyre.

Faber and Faber, London, and Harcourt Brace Jovanovich, Inc, Orlando,
Florida for the extracts from 'Little Gidding' from *Four Quartets* by T. S. Eliot.

**British Library Cataloguing in Publication Data**

Guiver, George
   Faith in momentum: the distinctiveness of the church.
   1. Anglicanism
   I. Title
   283

   ISBN 0–281–04468–6

Typeset by J&L Composition Ltd, Filey, North Yorkshire
Printed in Great Britain by
Courier International Ltd, Tiptree, Essex

*To the brethren of the
Abbey of St Matthias,
Trier*

# CONTENTS

# ACKNOWLEDGEMENTS

I owe a deep debt in what follows to Brother Harold SSF and the hermitage at Shepherd's Law, and to the integrity of its life expressed in prayer and work, in brick and stone, and in the necessity of pilgrimage amongst the world.

I am also greatly indebted to various brethren of the Community to which I belong for the help they have given, and the time they have generously spared, and particularly to the Community's Rule and Constitution Revision Committee for many insights on which this book draws.

I only hope that what follows does not let down those to whom it is indebted.

George Guiver CR
Mirfield 1989

# CHAPTER 1 *The Lion*

The small, bowed figure of a monk treads gently across the yard, scattering geese and chickens as he goes. He looks up momentarily into the deep azure of a cloudless Italian sky: who may understand the mind of God, who sets over our heads such a vision of order and peace, while here below humanity strives in turmoil, and all order seems as if at any moment it will pass away for ever? The old Roman Empire, which formed him in the rich fruits of its autumn, has slid with disastrous acceleration into oblivion, while the future promises little but chaos. The old man delays no longer, as there is work to be done.

Seated at a large lectern by the window he sharpens his pen in the sunlight, turning over and over again in his mind how to begin. Benedict, a gifted heir of five centuries of Christian asceticism, has decided upon a project, a distillation of the mystery which has called him and transformed him. Around his desk are propped the earlier attempts of others. But he hardly needs their books, he knows them all by heart, they are in his bones.

There is a knock on the door, and the guestmaster ushers in a young priest.

'Please take a seat', says Benedict with some reserve, while remaining standing himself, 'and tell me what I can do for you.'

The young man introduces himself as Marcus, and immediately embarks on a long and involved story about why he has been brought to sense a call to the monastic life. The monk listens with great patience while this tangled tale is told, trying not to make it appear obvious that he has heard it all before, many times, from so many ardent seekers after perfection. Finally comes the opportunity for him to respond.

'My son, I see that you are a good priest. Stay with your bishop, and tend the flock which God has put into your hand. That is what you are called to do. You aren't called to be a monk. Your present calling is a privilege to rejoice in.'

'But it's more difficult than that. I need a rule to live by. I need the discipline. We clergy have no rule such as that which guides your lives.'

'Ah yes, I know, but a rule is nothing to give your life for. The one which we follow at the moment is merely a deposit, a precipitate left by a living thing which is far greater. These rules are just like shavings left in the carpenter's shop. They are like the footprints left by someone you know well. A monastic rule is born from a life that is already lived. It is a distillation from a reality far too large to be imprisoned by pen and paper. Tell me, have you ever seen a lion?'

Marcus is the picture of disappointment. He looks down, shaking his head.

'But you have heard of him, in the Psalms, in the stories of the Judges, and in other parts of the Scriptures, in poems, hymns and prayers. And sometimes you can come across a picture of him, in the floors of old houses, or in old wall decorations. But none of them can give you any idea what it is like to meet a lion. Once in my childhood I saw one in a cage. He was magnificent, a thrilling sight, full of a life of his own, and he cared about nobody. He filled me with a terror I shall never forget. No picture can ever enable us to meet such a beast. The lion can inspire a painting to be created, but no painting can create a living lion. It's the same with the monastic life. The life gives birth to the rule. The rule can never give birth to the life.'

'But unless I become a monk first, how can I understand?'

'Monks have no monopoly of these things. What I have said of the monastery is true of the Church. She has a life of her own which can never be captured in any words. You can only look to one place for your rule, my dear son Marcus, and that is to the heart of the life of the Church. *There* is what you are to be seeking; it is not in rules. They are only rungs on the ladder, which leads to that great goal to which your eyes should be raised. Your heart is in the right place, Marcus, but have confidence in the Lord, and he will make of you a good priest.'

'Then why does a monastery have a rule? I don't understand.'

'There are some who say we shouldn't have one. It's a very dangerous thing to try to sketch out an intangible mystery in a few words. It can be mistaken for the mystery itself. We are always mistaking the part for the whole. Our rule just gives the rudiments, which point along the road. They are not the road itself. Our greatest rule is Scripture. What page of the Old and the New Testaments is not a most unerring rule of human life? The life of the nun or the monk is one of conversation with Scripture, a life of love, obedience and conversion. Don't be satisfied with seeking the signpost, Marcus; seek the road.'

And with that the interview comes to an end, having taken a course the young man had not expected. He scrambles down the mountainside under a cloud of disappointment, but as he progresses, he starts to pull himself together, and a determination grows in him not to be put off so easily.

The old man who has seemed to reject him now scribbles on, and continues to do so for several days. It is all flowing out much more spontaneously than he had expected, in fact he can hardly write quickly enough, and almost to his own surprise he eventually finds that he has written sufficient, and all that is left is to round it off. With characteristic modesty, he apologizes for this most humane document. The pen scratches out the final words on thick parchment:

> Whoever, therefore, you are who hasten to your heavenly country, fulfil first of all by the help of Christ this little rule for beginners. And then at length, under God's protection, you shall attain to those heights of virtue and wisdom which I have mentioned above.[1]

That little story raises a number of puzzling questions. The reader may be disappointed to leave Benedict and Marcus at this point, but we shall return to them again, and in the intervening space reflect on some issues which their encounter has opened up. These issues are as fundamental to the life of the Church today as they were in the sixth century. The purpose of this book is to point to something which is in certain ways veiled from our sight in the modern Church. Because it is in part veiled, and not open to view, the Church is in grave difficulty, graver perhaps than it may realize.

I wish to show, in however inadequate a way it may be, that the Church in many facets of its life, though not in all, is reduced to living off mere shavings of something greater, a reality which is its true birthright. It is good to eat the crumbs from the Master's table, but not so good to prefer the crumbs to the lavish feast he has prepared.

St Benedict rightly plays down his own rule. For without the greater reality which gave birth to the rule there can be no monastic life. Too much remains unsaid. This present book is not about the monastic life, but about the business of being Christians, in the family, in the city, in the village, or wherever people are living modern life as it is lived. So if you are beginning to think it is about obscurities of the monastic life, have no fear. Our concern is with the everyday Church, and a *something* which it seems to have lost.

It is always difficult to generalize about the Church, as things true in one place will not be true elsewhere, an exact description of one person will be inappropriate of another. And today the variety of ways in which the faith can be practised even within one denomination is greater than ever before. However, there is also a kind of unity to our age. Particular ages have their own flavour, and within a given period people holding widely different positions will all be affected and determined by the spirit of the time. In our own day conservatives, radicals, activists, contemplatives, and all the types you can imagine are deeply affected in ways they cannot see by the outlook of the age. How may that outlook be described? It can't. For one thing, it is far too complex, manifold, elusive, ambiguous, to be condensed into words. But it is also too close to us, too much a part of us, for us to see it for what it is. Nevertheless, in the pages that follow we shall see that certain dominant characteristics of our age are identifiable. So, to a certain extent, are some of the ways in which they condition the mentality of the Church, not always to its or anybody else's benefit.

In order to set the scene, it may be helpful to sketch out some dominant characteristics of the contemporary Church. This will inevitably be a bit of a caricature, but it will help to map out the specific kind of area we shall be examining.

If I had the opportunity to describe to St Benedict the Church to which I belong, perhaps I would first make clear that it is the Church of England, which has peculiar blessings and problems of its own, and of which I am proud and grateful to be a member. So my description would be very particular. But I know from experience that this Church is close enough to the other Churches of the West for much of what now follows to apply to them too. The Church of England's problems are not unique, but find their counterparts in all the mainstream Churches in Britain and abroad. So a good deal of what follows is just as relevant to them too.

I would begin by saying that it is a Church surrounded by luggage. It has brought with it from the past not only buildings, books, furniture, institutions and all manner of outward manifestations which condition its life, but also many attitudes from the past which it treasures, and others against which it strongly rebels. All of this is familiar enough not to need description. The important thing about it is that the luggage is one of the most fundamental things behind our present attitudes.

It lies, for instance, behind a remarkable reaffirmation of the incarnation in modern times. This does not seem to spring particularly from any resounding affirmation of the incarnation as historical event. Rather does it spring from a rebellion against one of the worst mistakes of our grandfathers, when they hived the Church off into a sterile world of its own, in which life and faith became separated. On the rebound we have embraced the 'world' with open arms. This reaction is well illustrated in this poem which reflects the thoughts of a sixteen-year-old girl:

> Priests, said my daughter, treat the Church like a cake,
> a marvellous cake. Made by a master baker.
> And unique. Unrepeatable.
> How wonderful, they say, examine the perfection.
> Enough for everyone, if only we dare share it.
>
> Priests, said my daughter, speak about it constantly,
> discuss its origins, ingredients, embellishments.
> They sigh over the icing cracks, regret decorations
> lost or crumbling. Irreplaceable, they say.
>
> Priests, said my daughter, are great preservers,
> keepers, guardians, curators reading recipes
> among their footnotes. And yet the master stands,
> apron and hands floured white, waiting
> with fresh bread for the poor.[2]

We have rejected such a cake, and turned all our enthusiasm upon the fresh bread. For us, God is to be identified in the things of everyday life. We meet him in our neighbour, we experience his otherness in the wonders of nature, we recognize his cross in the pain and the burdens of the poor, the oppressed, and those who have fallen victim to the destructive accidents of life. We recognize the stunning real-ness of everyday life and the presence of God within it, seeing that in the supermarket, the street, the hospital, the successful industry or the deprived home, the presence of God is as real as real can be. This perception leads to involvement and self-giving service of God's sons and daughters, whom he loves, and desires to cherish, and to give the gift of life in all its fullness. That realization about the incarnation, imperfectly as it is grasped, is enough to make us throw our hats in the air. It cannot be prized enough, and we are a long way yet from digesting it. As the *Faith in the City* report describes so well, the Church of England is a long way yet from discovering how 'ordinary working people' tick, and how different an expression of Christianity is needed among them (and always has been).

But these insights are also complemented by renewal in liturgy and in prayer and in rediscovery of much of the Christian ascetical tradition. Retreats, icons, spiritual journeys of discovery, prayer groups, and the like are now a 'growth industry'.

There is, however, some cause for disquiet. We find, first of all, the 'shot in the arm' syndrome. Prayer and liturgy are often seen as giving a shot in the arm to a Church whose main task is service of the world. Worship is like the pit in a car race. You stop off to be patched up quickly before speeding off again onto the track where the real race is taking place. The *Faith in the City* report, for instance, states that an outward-looking church 'must be aware that its locality is the first place in which God is to be both encountered and served'.[3]

Now, I wish to show two things about this: first, it is dubious theology—if God is not also to be found in the Church we may as well pack our bags; second, such a standpoint fails to produce the goods—far more than we realize, we are living off accumulated resources, throwing ourselves into the exhilarating mêlée of the modern world while living off our deposit account. This could be compared to gardening, where lack of proper composting and manuring means that after a few years the soil is exhausted. Examples are difficult to give, but it would be useful here to attempt one.

A man who has been formed by an old-fashioned parish in 'contemplative' and 'reverent' ways of worship, is now a parish priest. He has been acutely conscious of how alien this type of worship is for modern people, and so on Sundays he presides over a very informal, liberating act of worship, which aims to enable people to be joyful, to appreciate one another, and to take seriously the service of our neighbour and the mission of the Church. It seeks to proclaim that worship is enjoyable, and its purpose is to enable the Church to be at the service of the world. As a parish priest I have presided over worship which could be comparable, and would do so again without hesitation. However, these things are often taken too far, and come to dominate disproportionately. This is the mistake made by our hypothetical priest. He has, like many others, gone over the top, and the road he pursues is destined for trouble. The next generation of clergy will not have the benefit of the choice he has made. They will lack experience of what was good in the old, but will also lack the insights gained from suffering the bad in it. Much of modern worship is only sustainable by those who have also had solid experience of the old. The result: a younger generation which feels the lack, and is likely to end up seeking counterfeits of the real thing. One result is the so-called 'young fogey'. The 'shot in the arm' view, and talk of worship as primarily equipping for service in the world, are only true so far. On its own this approach undermines itself. It has to be set within a larger context.

It is often asserted as a self-evident fact of the gospel that the Church exists not for itself but for others. This is a good example of a truth which on its own is inadequate. It can only be a truth when it is held together with its opposite. Certainly a family which lives entirely for itself becomes not a family but a prison. But a family which lives entirely for other people cannot hope to remain a family either: its 'family-ness' will ultimately be dissipated. The Church can live for others only when it lives well with itself. This must surely be what the Lord envisaged when he prayed for his disciples that they may be one. One-ness has to be cultivated; it doesn't grow on trees. In just the same way God the Holy Trinity is the source of all love because the Trinity is held together in mutual love.

The modern Church so often has its eyes firmly set on the 'world', believing that God is behind us all the way, selflessly encouraging us to do his will for our neighbour. We believe in a self-effacing God, a self-effacing Church. We feel it important to put the Church in its place, to put worship in its place at the service of ourselves and others. But if that is what God's love is about, we should not blame anyone who might reply that he can keep it. Any fiancé worth his salt would say the same to his betrothed. Any child would have little respect for such a disinterested parent.

Our picture of God is so *theoretical*. Hence we are caught up in a cycle which can only lead to exhaustion, a Church starved of commerce with the Beloved, which, when asked to describe him, is embarrassed and stuck for something to say.

Our picture of the *Church* is similarly theoretical. Just as we undervalue our relationship with God, so we undervalue too the care that is needed in relating to each other. As I hope to show, our practice of one-ness falls far short of our talk about it. If the Church is to 'live well with itself' this will need much greater care over personal relationships and over the way different groups relate with each other. The gospel does not sit happily with a body which contains within itself enduring conflicts of interest; it continually points beyond them. If the Church is to take itself seriously this should not be confused either with that 'institutional self-interest' which is rightly challenged in the *Faith in the City* report. A critical search for its true treasures will mean digging down beyond the flat fixities of the Establishment.

Finally, the Church can only 'live well with itself' if it lives well with the world. The above remarks are simply a corrective to the current tendency to allow the world to set too much of the agenda. The Church cannot live without the insights of the world. Theology, for instance, has to start where people are, and follow the age-old principle of sound methods of learning: to trace from the familiar to the unfamiliar, from everyday reality to the truths it points towards.

All of this would suggest a slight but important adjustment to the position we have criticized. It could be put in this way: the Church cannot exist primarily for itself, and it cannot exist primarily for the world. It is when the two dimensions engage, each in its complete integrity, that something greater than both comes to birth.

Taking for granted that enough people are already convinced of the 'world' side of the equation, the following chapters seek to tease out what we might mean by saying the Church should also take seriously its own internal dimension. We shall do this with a particular eye to the question, 'Why does the Church have to contain so many things which to outsiders (and even to Christians themselves) appear odd and peculiar?'

Why do two friends play cards? For the pleasure of it. But wherein lies the pleasure? Perhaps in the challenge, and the sense of competition. But why should that be enjoyable? Ultimately, it must be because you are coming to grips with another person. A game of cards is distinguished from playing patience in that the game is raised into the more quickened level of *relationships*. Games are a way of relating. Vehicles for loving, hating, avenging, delighting-in an Other. A competitive game can touch deep layers of that onion which is our psyche. It can be a vehicle for becoming more-than-ourselves through a specially channelled way of relating to other persons.

This is true not only of games but also, for instance, of dancing, going for a drink, music-making with friends, many kinds of common endeavour from organizing a garden fête to running a trade union or board meeting. The job in hand inevitably involves and affects personal relationships.

Sometimes we evolve very elaborate 'card games' to serve particular purposes. The British House of Commons is a good example. Since its proceedings began to be broadcast, much of the British public has come to see it as a bear pit, a chaos of gut-noises, unseemly dog-fights, and the swelling roar of an animal herd. While it would be naive to suppose that much of the House's business is not cut-throat, unscrupulous and unedifying, this should not be confused with the strange but very effective mechanics of parliamentary procedure. Over the centuries this has evolved into a versatile 'card game' which enables rapid and simultaneous communication. Interjections, symbolic waves, stylized formal address, the sometimes heaving polyphony of massed voices, enable many things to be said, and understood, at once. Such a lively and effective game-for-communication should not be judged simply on the basis of its misuse. It is a game of cards which enables many things to be said which could be said in no other way.

In order to refine this down a little, it will be helpful now to turn to a specifically Christian 'card game', the life of religious communities. This is a strange game indeed, often misunderstood by outsiders, and yet it can shed particularly clear light on some aspects of how the Church is called to be the Church. Here is an example from the community to which I belong. The mother house is set in spacious grounds bounded by a stone wall. If I wish to go outside the wall, say to the Co-op, our custom is that I ask the prior (unless it be between 2 and 4 o'clock in the afternoon!). The prior invariably says Yes. How ridiculous and trivial: a grown man running to ask permission for such a small thing. Surely that is to behave like babies. It is to inculcate a child–parent relationship, encouraging immaturity and dependence. Such things might be said.

These criticisms fail to see the true issues. The brethren agree that the face value counts for little, but they know that behind this trivial transaction lies an extensive hinterland. It is this hinterland which comes into play when I ask: 'May I go to the shop?' It is a hinterland so vital to the community's life that the prior and the head of the whole community have like anyone else to ask permission on such occasions.

This little ritual is, first of all, an acting-out of the fact that I have committed myself to community, life and limb. I am no longer simply I. We are brethren. I have put myself into the hands of my brothers, as each of them has put himself into our hands. In the making of this request, I and the prior are acting that out, writing it across the cosmos. And through acting out such a mysterious thing as brotherhood we send our roots further down into it. Connected with that is another thing. Life in our community aims at stability. That is a technical term, and part of its meaning is that we renounce flitting from one thing to the next, just as we have renounced choosing whom we shall have for company. All religious communities are strange, motley assortments of people. We are committed to staying with each other, and that means no running away from odd habits, odd relationships, odd smells, and company which is not always congenial. In the same way we have to 'stay with' ourselves, reducing the distractions and the escapes. Stability means staying on the spot where you are standing. This spot may be, for instance, a feeling of loneliness or boredom. Stability means not to run to something else, but to take this present moment as the most real thing that can happen to you, and bore down further into it. Thus we uncover layer after layer of the mystery of this 'card game', and become, if he should will it, less ready to run away from God. So the brother knocking on the prior's door is laying down a hand in the card game of stability, acting out his and the community's ideals in a mime which will leave neither participant unchanged.

Those are two departments of the hinterland behind this small custom of a religious community. There are yet more departments to it, touching on such matters as the art of listening, the educating of pride, or the sustaining of order, which need not be gone into here. What I have described should be sufficient to show that there are stylized acts and transactions in human relationships whose face value is apparently negligible, but behind them stretch hinterlands of accumulated meaning. The purpose of the action is to acknowledge and give honour to that complex of interrelated values.

Now it is possible for religious communities and for Churches to lose sight of the hinterland which lies behind inherited practices. In recent years religious communities, partly due to a desire to make the right response to the onslaught of rapid changes taking place in the modern world, have often lost contact with some of their inherited wisdom. So a weakened understanding of this notion of hinterland meant in the 1960s and 70s that a number of practices in the life of religious communities were modified or abandoned to the detriment of the life. Many things certainly had to be changed, but in practice some which deserved retention were lost, while others which were inadequate were mistakenly retained. We are thus not arguing against change, but in favour of change based on more adequate grounds.

It would be useful to ask what is inadequate about the grounds, because the changes that have gone on in recent years have been experienced by the whole Church, as everyone will know well, and therefore answering the question may shed light for all of us, not just for those who live in religious communities. It could probably be said that many practices in the life and worship of the Church which have been abandoned in recent years were abandoned either on grounds of common sense, or because of recent theological insights, or because they did not accord with the spirit of the times. All of these are valid and important considerations, and need to be taken into account. Yet without also considering the 'card game' factor any change we make may be open to serious charges of inconsistency.

In a monastery, for example, certain formalities may be abolished as being outdated or unnatural. But if that is the case, why not abolish the lot? The whole thing is unnatural, and when simply judged against canons of common sense or the spirit of the times, the whole monastic life must be shown to be patent nonsense in its entirety. However, if you accept, as you must if you are a monk or a nun, that the thing is a carefully calculated game with a serious end in view, a 'card game' carefully adjusted with fine checks and balances, painfully evolved through centuries of mistakes and revelations, then you must take very seriously indeed every single aspect of it whenever change is being mooted, aware of the vast and to some extent invisible nature of the hinterland.

Note particularly why I have chosen here the image of a game of cards. Many will find it uncongenial. A card game is essentially rigid in its rules and competitive in spirit. It seems to be superficial and stuck, a rigmarole for whiling away the time. A card game *can* be all of those things. But it can also be a powerful and gripping way of relating to another or to a group, engaging such vital levels that it leaves us pleased, refreshed and changed. This is largely through the come-and-go with other people which it enables.

In exactly the same way in the life of the Church, rituals, routines and conventions can seem rigid, nonsensical and childish. This may, however, be because we fail to see their capacity to foster the chemistry of being human, a capacity that can transcend more ordinary ways of relating to each other and to God.

In the renewal of the life of religious communities many practices have been rejected on the basis of their face value, with little investigation of what might have been the nature of the hinterland lying behind an apparently wooden or even daft appearance.

Things true of the monastery are equally true of the diocese and the parish. Many attitudes which were revered or sacrosanct have been adapted or abandoned, often for justified pastoral and theological reasons. For instance, it is now normal to be able to have coffee in church, to call the clergy by their Christian names, to be informal, relaxed and chatty in worship rather than recollective and reverent; clergy often abandon clerical dress, while other members of various types of ministry turn out in church in all imaginable kinds of creation under the sun. Many of these things were needed.

Often the problem is that we have gone for replacement of one thing by another, rather than attempting to keep both.

Some old ways may deserve to go. That is not the question. What is at question is not change, but the grounds on which we base it. In the 1960s it was rightly diagnosed that change was needed. However, in the secular world, high-rise blocks of flats proved to be little improvement on terraced houses. In the Church too it is not easy to say that change has been what it should have been: much of the change has involved the turfing out of the remnants of our 'card games'. We can see in these things, whether in church or in secular life, something which might be called the 'overdone rebound'. We react from a mistake, but in the process tar many good things with the same brush through failing to distinguish the issues clearly enough. The same can be said of something we noted in Chapter 1, a tendency in the Church of England to reject seeing the Church as a primary revelation of God's presence because we associate all of that with a blinkered 'institutional self-interest' which has let people down.

So in our processes of renewal we saw the Church as a battered old car. We gave it a reconditioned carburettor (new liturgical texts), a couple of retreaded tyres (improved finances) and a few other replacement parts, and then expected it to zoom along the fast lane. But the petrol tank still leaks, the transmission is loose and the steering dangerous, because important parts have been looked at briefly and then thrown away after a shrug of the shoulders. Nor is that all. The mechanics don't seem to be aware of the fact that this is an enchanted car. It's not at all certain what help new carburettors and tyres can be in these circumstances. And as for those outdated parts we threw away, they may have been more important than we thought. The Church is holy, and it is a mystery, a worldly, sinful body of people who have all around them, if they will see, a vital hinterland. We sometimes see the Church naively as merely a convenient machine. If it starts to stall, all we need to do is fiddle with the parts a bit and it will go better. Synods, committees and special officers for this and that soldier away at their maintenance work, but it is a good question whether in at least some of the things which absorb their energies they are doing justice to themselves and the Body of Christ. While all this work goes on with the best of intentions, vital areas of the Church's vocation lie ignored and neglected. One example must suffice here.

All Christians need 'card games' to play with God. In this domain in Britain the scene is one of devastation, its roots going back four hundred years to the Reformation. This becomes immediately clear to anyone who encounters that Church which is commonly known as Orthodox, the Church of the Byzantine rite. Recently a service from a Moscow church was broadcast on British television. Our first view was of the gate opening onto the street and the path leading from it to the church. People stopped by the graves of relatives and friends to pray and make the sign of the cross. Once in church they prostrated themselves several times on the ground, and then visited the icons: the icon of the day, Our Lord, the Blessed Virgin, St Nicholas, and other favourite saints and theological symbols, making the sign of the cross and bestowing a familiar kiss. Then there were candles to light. Then names of relatives and friends in need to write on a piece of paper to be offered in the prayers. There were offerings of bread, grapes, wine and oil, an inheritance from the love-feasts of the early Christians. And so it went on, in a way that will be familiar to some.

What is happening here? Superstition? The worship of idols? Peasant folk custom? No indeed, it is more than that. It is worship of the living God manifested in Jesus Christ and proclaimed by his saints, worship which finds its place in these simple actions themselves, but fans out from them into the eternal.

Of the many other observations which could be made on this, one deserves our attention here. It sounds inappropriate to talk of card games, but the striking thing about this Russian one is that everyone is provided with a kind of 'kit', an ensemble of actions, gestures, objects and symbols with which each person can have an exchange with God. As I have pointed out elsewhere,[4] most clergy are ideas-people, at home with the abstract. But the vast majority of the population are action-people, at home with the concrete. Clergy ask the question: 'What must be believed?', where most laity are wanting rather to ask, like the young man in the Gospels: 'What must I do?' Here these good Muscovites have their kit, and it stands them in good stead, through thick and thin, both clergy and laity together. Other Churches have corresponding 'kits'. The Roman Catholic Church still has a very rich one, although it is looking a little battered. Anglicans are in a very different state. For them there is nothing, or next to nothing (except perhaps in some parishes of a Catholic tradition). The Reformation took away people's 'kit' and tried to foist an intellectual religion on them in its place. It has been said that the Book of Common Prayer was written (can the verb 'written' be used of liturgy anyway?) by dons and bishops for dons and bishops. Not surprisingly the people were first marginalized and then repelled by a gospel reduced to wordy monologues and moral precepts.

The Church of England lost the common people a long time ago. In the process it evolved a range of gifts which are clearly God-given, and which we may summarize here as the Anglican genius and the Anglican ethos. In a most curious way these gifts have come to be the property largely of the clergy and a small proportion of committed and educated laity. The vast majority of ordinary worshippers would not recognize many of these gifts, and certainly have little experience in exercising them. Unlike most other Churches, many of Anglicanism's most unique gifts are not shared commonly by both clergy and laity together. That, at least for the present writer, is one symptom of the lack of a framework which would enable the common people to see the Church of England as their Church. Mercifully the Prayer Book's disincarnational wordiness came to be mitigated by a good dash of Victorian vulgarity, and has now at last been further unloosed through liturgical renewal and fuller participation by all in the liturgy. But people need more.

There are, for instance, many people in the Church who need formal liturgy and accepted devotional practices. They need them because they are not cut out for discussion groups, nformal encounters, or what is reckoned to be spontaneous living. Many people tick in this way. It is almost, if you like, a response to Christ and his Church that can only be made obliquely, by means of tokens of regard. Such faith is in no way inferior to that of people who have the gift of being outgoing, informal, loquacious or even invasive. It is simply different. Knowing when this needs to be acknowledged in people, and when it needs to be challenged, is a very difficult thing to gauge. All of us, clergy, and laity, need a Church which is not ashamed to play apparently superficial games with God, games which, while simple in themselves, vibrate outwards, enabling us to resonate with things beyond our sight.

I have been fascinated by these things for a number of years, and I hope the reader will forgive me if I become a little auto-biographical here, in order to elucidate what I mean. Many years ago now I was once participating in a rather elaborate form of evening office in a small, remote religious house, when suddenly the penny dropped about the daily office. It dawned on me that here was an external palaver which achieved more than was visible on the surface.

About the same time I was on one occasion sitting in a hairdresser's overhearing two people talking on the pavement outside, when it struck me that exactly the same thing was going on: an external, ritualized palaver following a predictable course, but achieving something beyond our sight, a communication of greater value than was externally visible. I also had the feeling that the actual talking and gesturing were more than a series of tokens— in some way they were an intimate part of the communication itself.

Shortly after that I found myself at the Sunday liturgy in a Romanian Orthodox monastery, experiencing a Westerner's shock and amazement at the sheer physicality of this colourful throng of people praying with vivid physical signs and energetic gestures of the body. I discovered the formal, old-fashioned traditions of Romanian villages, and the entrancing humanity of their way of life—a lovely and loving people, saints and rogues, good and evil, dancing out their dance in elaborate external patterns of living. A pre-modern society with all its simplicity and drawbacks, but in touch with something about themselves that I was not in touch with about myself. That 'something' we shall meet again later on, but for the present I only want to draw attention to the formal external observances and manners of this society, and a sense of the hinterland that lies behind them.

Some years later again, I had the experience of joining a religious community, and realizing the extent to which faithfulness to formalities that sometimes might even seem downright potty can enable a group of people to embark on a spiritual journey together, who in any other circumstances might soon be at one another's throats. Yet again it was brought home to me that external practices can have a vital relation to inner processes.

These thoughts have itched away in me for so long that it was a very joyful moment when I came across a book devoted to this very phenomenon, Fergus Kerr's *Theology after Wittgenstein*.[5] The analysis presented there corresponds so closely to what I have concluded from experience, that I shall now draw on it in order to take further what needs to be said about 'card games'.

Kerr shows that any talk of inner depths to our person is meaningless if detached from the apparently superficial encounters of every day. We have inherited some very deeply-rooted assumptions about something which might be called an 'inner self'. Wittgenstein sets out to show how these assumptions are erroneous. A good example is taken from the passage in Augustine's *Confessions* in which he describes his infancy:

> Gradually I realized where I was, and I decided to display my wishes to those who might fulfil them, and I could not because my wishes were inside and they were outside, and powerless to get inside my mind by any of their senses. So I shook my limbs and varied my voice, the few signs like my wishes that I could manage, as well as I could, but they were really not very similar.[6]

Child psychology has shown us that such a picture is not only seriously inadequate, but completely mistaken. Our development as a person depends on our progressive relating to others within the community of society. And it is primarily through *language* and through *actions* that we learn to think and to marshal our feelings. Without language and without commerce with others it would all remain inchoate: our 'inner self' would not come to birth.

In order to make completely clear what I am trying to say, I shall proceed to put Wittgenstein's insights as starkly as I can. We are so confirmed in our attitudes that only shock therapy can put a dent in them, and only by putting the issues in a stark and simple light is it possible to show up the inadequacies of our accepted understandings. I should add that this is my interpretation of Kerr's interpretation of Wittgenstein's writings. What is presented here is not an exposition of Wittgenstein, but a presentation of one strand in his thought which puts in vivid terms something which I already believed to be true.

Wittgenstein shows to devastating effect that all which is most meaningful and most real in our lives derives from our commerce with others. So we take on board the tools which society has evolved for bringing order out of our chaos. Without the tools which society has handed on to us, we would be unable to think, unable to develop as persons. One of the most important of these tools is language. Language is so important that without it no thought can take place. Furthermore, what we say does not merely reflect our inner thoughts: it *is* what we are thinking. Anyone who has ever attempted to write their thoughts on paper can testify to the way our thinking comes to birth and grows as we write. The writing is far from a mere aid to the inner process. It *is* the process. So we can sometimes open our mouth on a subject before we have become clear what we think about it—but our ideas take shape as we speak. This is why listening is the most important part of counselling. The other person doesn't so much need advice or guidance as an opportunity for putting things into words. Often a counsellor can be thanked profusely, when in fact they have said hardly a word in the whole interview. Simply by being there as the person they were, they gave their 'client' an opportunity to pour it all out in words. Why is it so helpful? Because in part, that is how we think, by putting things into words. The verbalizing *is* our thought, whether done audibly, or in our head. Hence the achievements of psychotherapy, in which we talk our way through towards greater perception, and in which we find that all obstacles to it have been planted in us by events and experiences that have pierced us from the outside.

What I say is what I am. This isn't to say that I can not sometimes be thinking things which are contrary to what I am saying audibly. It means that my thoughts always take the form of language, which I have received from outside. The heart of life lies not in some invisible 'depths' where things 'most important' to me lurk, striving for expression. The innermost me is not a hermit in my head: the heart of my life lies in the commerce which takes place between me and the exterior world. It is in *actions* that I come to be, that I grow, that I live life with the greatest sense of realness.

This does not mean of course that there are no depths, or that there is no inner reflection. Of course we have inner depths. The question is: How did they get inside me? We assume the essential person to be within, burrowing outwards, as in diagram (a) opposite. For Wittgenstein, however, the depths are excavated from the outside inwards (see diagram (b)).

Our depths have received form and shape through the interaction we have had with the world around us. This is a fundamental fact of psychology. It should not, however, be misunderstood: we are not speaking here of a crude determinism, in which we are merely stamped and determined by our environment. There is no narrow

18

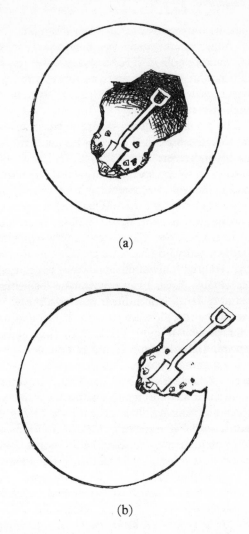

(a)

(b)

form of collectivism either, in which the individual is accorded little value. Each individual is totally unique, with his or her unique gifts and personal will.

We are speaking here, rather, of the chemistry of our commerce with our environment, through which our individuality is given structures. Within them it can come to birth out of chaos. It is in the 'card games' of life that the crucial essence of human consciousness is decisively established, not in some independent inner being, who observes the 'outside world' as a spectator. The myth of the soul as imprisoned in the body was condemned at the Second Council of Constantinople in 553, but has been widely believed in ever since. That which we experience as 'inner' is to a great extent the *product* of commerce with the world; never, as we suppose, does it *precede* such commerce.

This could be put another way. We are all conscious of ourselves in a way that we are conscious of no other person. I am permanently landed with the awareness that I am me, and that my 'me-ness' seems to go back into depths beyond my sight. Often thoughts and feelings which are beyond words emerge from those depths. We are not saying that none of that exists. What we are saying is that this cannot simply be seen as unprocessed, quintessential me. It has all been woven in the loom of life, its weft and warp being relationships with others and with God.

One of the essential roots of our mistake is our relegation of the body to a secondary place, as an unfortunate incidental necessity for the sustaining of the mind. Such downgrading of the body is ingrained in our culture, leaving us with an inability to recognize that our body is essential to our being. Both mind and body make us what we are. Indeed, some of the profoundest layers of our being have been laid by physical participation in some action or other, such as a kiss, a car accident, gardening, listening to music, or a fight. Our lopsided tradition of isolating the mind is typified in a saying of Pascal: 'Man is only a reed, the weakest in nature, but he is a thinking reed.' Wittgenstein recoiled from this with strong words: 'It is humiliating to appear like an empty tube which is simply inflated by a mind.'[7] He found it humiliating because he had come to see that his body was an essential part of the personality. He found himself being accused of being a lesser being.

To live is to act, and for action we need our bodies. 'What constitutes us as human beings is the regular patterned reactions that we have to one another.'[8] In such interaction body and mind are a unity. Our life is full of 'regular patterned reactions', which fill our day chock-a-block. The mind may sometimes play a minor part in them. So for most of the day we relate to people around us without great concentration on what we are doing. We would be intolerable if we concentrated on everyone with our total being while we spoke to them. 'There may be nothing at all going on in your mind', Wittgenstein observes, 'and still you may not talk like a parrot.'[9]

F. Hölderlin can sum this up in a phrase profound in its simplicity, when he speaks of 'the conversation which we are'.[10] There is a strongly entrenched myth, Kerr says, that there has to be an element of 'reflection or deliberation in every respectable human action. Otherwise actions fail to be intelligent or free—and the people in whose daily lives reflection and deliberation seldom occur drop into the margins of history.'[11]

This kind of prior reflection is, however, a specialist activity, appropriate only in certain fields. It is important in designing a house, but has to be kept in its place in human relating, or piano playing, where spontaneous, all-round response with the whole person is the stuff of life. 'Why do I not satisfy myself', asks Wittgenstein, 'that I still have two feet when I want to get up from a chair? There is no why. I simply don't. This is how I act.'[12] Exactly the same can be said about a great deal of prayer and worship. The outward observances of Russian Orthodox peasants in church can be patronized as mindless rigmarole, when in fact they are a living of life in its profoundest depths. We frequently hear warnings against the danger of mindless repetition in prayer. But to assume that prayer without 'inner reflection' cannot be true prayer is, ultimately, heresy. The battle against Gnosticism has been waged since New Testament times, but it has been alive and healthy in the Western Church for many centuries, in a widespread 'disavowal of the mundane world of conversation and collaboration in which human life consists'.[13]

Observe yourself as you go through the day, particularly when you relate to people at a very human and personal level, greeting somebody warmly, or discussing this or that problem or enthusiasm. Where is the seat and root of your engagement? Is it way back, down in the depths? Not often. Normally it is in the tip of your tongue, the glance of your eyes and the wave of your hand.

Jesus, in criticizing 'vain' repetitions, was speaking as a Jew. He did not mean that the 'mind' had to be fully engaged; he meant the heart. For the Jew, body and soul are one entity. But in our inherited Western culture the body is held to be inferior to some gaseous essence which is superior, and destined to outlast it, as the essential, 'inner' person. The Old and New Testaments insist however that the body is as essential in the makeup of the person as

21

is the soul. In Kerr's words: 'To hold that "the ego is mental" is to place oneself in the long . . . tradition of isolating the spiritual from the physical.'[14] So Wittgenstein asks, Where are the foundations of our religion? In the feelings? No. In the reason? No. What is foundational is *action*. It therefore comes as no surprise that Christian tradition has seen the heart of the Church's life as being closely associated with the eunharistic action.

The reader may well be rebelling against all these outrageous claims, but he or she should take that as an indicator of how ingrained (and unbiblical) our misconceptions are. Wittgenstein himself realizes how tough they are. It will certainly take much more than my brief digest to convince many of you who are reading this book. Wittgenstein believed it needs a slow therapy. For him, 'We may not *terminate* a disease of thought. It must run its natural course, and *slow* cure is all-important.'[15]

Often the error of what we say becomes clear once we analyse it, or if we watch what we are saying and thinking. Observe yourself sometimes, and see what words you use, what models of human nature you presuppose. If you have been affected at all by the ideas of Wittgenstein, you will be shocked at the things you find yourself saying. Look, for instance, at our misuse of the biblical word 'faith'. In the Gospels faith is primarily an action, a response to a person, a gift which enables us to follow Jesus. It is used in other ways, but this is central. In the phrase 'the Christian faith', however, we tend too easily to limit 'faith' to mean merely a structure of abstract propositions. Constantly we speak of 'the Christian faith' in this way, and talk about it all resting on what people 'believe'. But it is not only to do with mere beliefs. Jesus calls us to get up and follow, he calls us to act and live in a certain way. When people say, 'My beliefs are so-and-so', they are giving a relatively useless piece of information. 'So what?' we could well reply. This is not a downgrading of doctrine. Doctrine is action in response to Jesus: in breaking bread, in attending in silence, in washing the feet of others. And close on follow the reflection and the formulation.

The word 'faith' is used today in all kinds of ways. We should listen to how we use it, and be particularly careful not to limit it to mean simply the propositional content of the gospel. We need to be much more chary of simply calling Christianity a 'faith'. A more biblical term might be 'the Christian Way', for to follow this way is to be engaged not merely in our minds, but in our bodies, our affections, our whole persons.

Another example: if someone goes on retreat 'to enter into my inner depths and reflect on the things most important to me', he or she is in fact giving a classic description of hell, where individuals are entirely turned in upon themselves. Whence comes this conscious, self-reflective 'inner' world? Was it there in the pram? If not, did it come to birth through some spontaneous pregnancy? No. It was born through commerce with the world, and the natural place for it to find healthy life is there. A person, therefore, who goes on retreat is not retiring into self, but will continue conversations which the world and God have initiated. Retreatants are not retiring from commerce, but *shifting* the commerce to another arena for relating to God, and the fact that God is there to participate in such action is demonstrated by the fact that hermits (and retreatants) do not usually go mad.

In our society a supposedly autonomous individual is taken as the measure of reality. If, as it seems, there is no such thing as an individual who is autonomous, no wonder that we have so much unhappiness and fragmentation. The sovereign self has been awarded a 'right' to be itself. But it can never find that 'self-ness' which it seeks, because that can only be found in collaborative action in community. So we pursue a fruitless search for a 'fulfilment' which is only to be found in the opposite direction to the one in which we are travelling. If I seek merely personal fulfilment I will never find it. This is because fulfilment is only found through accepting the uncomfortable hurly-burly of life with others. This entirely accords with the Gospel, where we are assured that we find ourselves only through losing ourselves.

At the everyday level, this can take quite humdrum forms. For our inner life we are dependent to a large extent on what Wittgenstein calls *Lebensformen*, which may be translated 'life-forms'.[16] These are such things as language, the communication games of our culture, established patterns of behaving, reacting, communicating, in short, things which above we have called 'card games'. When any Christian performs a move in a card game such as lighting a candle, venerating an icon, or keeping the sometimes strange rules of a religious community, he or she recognizes that such things have a significance beyond their face value. They have a hinterland. But in addition the person performing the act is acknowledging that such a hinterland does not lurk in some hidden shadows, but is really present in the act itself. Just as, when I embrace someone I love, I don't do it because the act 'means' something. The meaning is in the very doing of the act. I don't think to myself, 'I am putting my arms around so-and-so, and this is intended to mean a, b and c.' In fact, it is precisely when such acts are too premeditated that they can lose their power and their ability to convince. My thinking, intentions and feelings are all part and parcel of the act, they come to birth in it. When we reflect upon such actions, we recognize that that is exactly how it feels.

It is almost impossible to do justice to this aspect of Wittgenstein's insights in such a brief space as this, and if the reader, as is quite likely, still bristles with questions, he or she should read Fergus Kerr's book. But I suspect there will be many others for whom, like myself, this summary puts into words things which they have long felt and wanted to express.

One little remark of Kerr's about the ancient Greeks puts much of it in a nutshell: for them 'the depth of the world is on the surface'.[17] So the depth of Christianity has its roots in *action* which takes place in the visible world, be it acts of love and service, or the stylized acts of the Christian 'dance', the 'card games' of the Church and her traditions of prayer. In both cases, we are taken down into our depths by the performing of the very actions.

When I befriend someone who is terminally ill, or make time to listen to a stranger's problems, there I find the inner depths of following Christ. When we sing evensong together or act out the Holy Week ceremonies, there is Christ's profundity, in the encounter with him in the very action. It is through these exterior things that we are deepened, far more than by personal, inner reflection. The latter is only able to function at all by drawing on such exterior actions. It is through these *actions* that we are able to pursue a journey which is inwards all the way.

It is no contradiction, therefore, to assert with age-old tradition that the journey to God is a journey inwards. At the centre lies not the essential me, not the hermit in the head; at the centre towards which this inward journey struggles waits God himself.

The paradox is that God is also very much there in the world outside us, waiting to speak to us as we engage in its hurly-burly. My presentation of Wittgenstein has been necessarily stark, and we should not leave it without setting it in a fuller perspective. The interaction between internal and external has a further dimension to it: it is a permanent two-way chemistry. Or perhaps it is like a yo-yo which works in both directions, travelling a little further each time. I have of course simplified an immensely complex subject, deliberately emphasizing some things in order to put them in a clear light. This way I have hoped to show that the person is rather like a seed coming to birth through commerce with all that is outside itself. I have left aside many things which also have a claim on us, such as the absolute address which God makes to the individual (not to be confused with some address which an autonomous individual is supposed to be able to make to God). My hope is that this 'therapy' may work like a dose of salts, so that the reader, while realizing there is much more to the matter than has been said here, will nevertheless find that his or her perspectives on life have undergone an important shift.

If, for example, we consider the ills of the Church today, we can begin to see that they are partly due to a terrible poverty in 'life-forms', 'card games' which provide the dance of interrelating through which we become most profoundly what we are. Many Christians are biased against this by the ingrained Western illusion of the autonomous inner self. But the self can only be found in fragments if sought in separation from interrelating in the Body of Christ. Christians need 'life-forms', 'card games' in which they can relate to each other and to God, a 'kit' of activities, understandings and rigmaroles in which our profoundest selves can be brought to birth.

Where may these things be found? The solution to this problem is easier than might seem. Part of the task is not to create a new vocabulary of activities, but to make more of all that we already have, by taking more seriously the liturgy of the Church, and its outward paraphernalia and customs and traditions. All we need to do is treat things more carefully, rediscover the traditional ways in which they have been understood, and generally accord to what we already do in liturgy and prayer a greater importance. Prayer can be informal and still transcendent. Worship can be relaxed and have a family atmosphere and still be mysterious and have a profound sense of history. In a sense we need to stay with what we have, but discover its hinterland. Then in supplementing these with other things we need to be clear about what we are doing. If we need 'card games' in order to live the gospel to the full, we now have to address the question: Will *any* card game do?

# CHAPTER 3 *The Vine*

Time and again as we proceed we shall find ourselves stumbling across a problem that seems to pop up everywhere we look: the tip of the iceberg being mistaken for the whole. We have seen in the previous chapter that external practices can mistakenly be taken at face value only. We can make similar mistakes when we ask: 'Who is performing it?' On the face of it, the people in the Moscow church are each doing their own thing. Each person is doing what he or she chooses to do, ringing their own changes from a common fund of stock practices. But this last observation gives the lie to this assumption. They are not simply doing their own thing. Every person does it in a unique way, but fundamentally the agent is not the individual. It is the community. Who is kissing the icon of Our Lord? The community. Who is asking leave of the prior? The community (and the response too is the community's).

This is not theological wishful thinking. It is a fact of life. When I wear a red poppy in November I am a miniature version of the nation, part of a common, even if not unanimous, action. And for many people still, Remembrance Sunday makes us very conscious not only of the nation. It makes us aware of the dead, and of very vivid and traumatic experiences in the nation's recent past. When I wear a poppy, I embody the nation as it wears the red poppy. When I pray, it is the community that prays.

To some this may sound like a kind of religious communism: up with the collective, down with the individual. Not so at all. It is only in community that the person can fully become an individual. The weaker the community, the more shadowy we become as individuals. Modern society proves this for us at every turn. Lack of community leads to lack of meaning in life, lack of community spirit, together with a paradoxical conformity and herd instinct, and a tendency to treat people as things. Community may be more constricting and more demanding, but it is what we were made for, and without it we are shadows of ourselves.

In order to appreciate this in its proper context, we need to turn to biblical imagery. Jesus in St John's Gospel gives us the image of the vine, and this is of great help here, because so far in this argument we have seen the Church as being only of the present moment. The Church of the 1990s is one snapshot in a 2000-year-old photograph album. We don't care much for the others—just for the 1990 one. The Lord's image of the vine won't let us get away with that.

The vine is one of the most magical of symbols, suggesting abundant life, eternity and bliss. Frequently in the Old Testament the vine is Israel: 'You cleared the ground for it. It took deep root and filled the land. The mountains were covered with its shade, the mighty cedars with its branches; it sent out its branches to the sea, and its shoots to the river.'[18]

The vine came to symbolize, among other things, the Messiah who was to come, and so it is no surprise to see Jesus taking this up to refer to himself: 'I am the true vine, you are the branches. He who abides in me, and I in him, he it is that bears much fruit ... I am the true vine, and my Father is the vine dresser.'[19]

Just as the image of the vine as Messiah came to be transferred to Jesus, so the image of Israel as the Lord's vine is naturally transferred to the Church. The Body of Christ with its many members and the vine with its many branches are two facets of the same thing: Christ abiding in his people in such a way that they are the Church, his presence on earth.

It is also a symbol of the Church's continuity. The vine is a symbol of the Church in time. So when we gather together to celebrate the liturgy we are united with Christ and his apostles, the early Fathers, saints and ordinary believers down all the centuries until today. Here we have a strong sense of the Church's unity in time. The other kind of unity, the geographical kind, is easy to grasp. Christians in Margate, Peking and Honolulu are one Body, the Church Catholic. But this second aspect of the catholicity of the Church, its unity through time, is not so easy for us to live with. We say, 'Yes, we believe what they believed. But they are dead. They cannot help fight our battles today.' And we say so not wholly rejecting the past, because we do reverence it. We all have things in the Christian past which we value. But at the level of our guts it is difficult to give a great deal of importance to the past, to history.

Take St Odo of Cluny. He is someone most of us will not have heard of, so we are not inclined to take him seriously. Added to this is another discouragement; he is dead. So are his daily worries, his daily tasks and his particular vintage of Christian belief. They are all dead. Yet if they are, and if all that means anything to ordinary Christians in every age of the past, if all are dead, 'then we of all people are the most to be pitied'. For 'God is not the God of the dead but of the living.' They are not dead. Death has been conquered. 'The communication of the dead is tongued with fire beyond the language of the living.'[20] The Church is a living vine whose sap passes through centuries of time, to bring life to us and send us on to the future. How?

If we are cut off from the past we have no future. A living future is only possible if it is the making new of a living inheritance. Look, for instance, at the history of painting. Memling, say, would have been impossible had there been no Flemish school of painting in the Middle Ages; and before that, manuscript illumination, and so on backwards through the stages through which European painting has passed. It would have been impossible for a Flemish painting of a religious scene to pop up out of nowhere. And the more familiar we are with the story of painting the more we will understand the works of Memling.

Or let us take an icon. It would have been impossible to create it had there not gone before it the Roman Empire with its particular forms of figurative painting. And the step from late Roman art to Byzantine is very small. European art traces its roots backwards past the Roman Empire through tracts of time beyond our imagining, to the first paintings and scratches on wood and rock. Art is a vine which cannot go forward except as a branch growing from what preceded it. Even, as in some modern art, when it rebels against its inheritance, the shape of this rebellion is closely determined by the character of that which it tries to turn from.

If that is the case, what about you? Your particular ways of thought, particular ways in which you twitch your nose—where did they come from? An Italian or a Japanese may find them baffling or comic, but for you and me they are normal, inherited ways of dancing the dance of life, mannerisms and modes of thought which have been passed on to us from centuries ago, so familiar that we think they are just bland, normal and inevitable. We are products of the past, and the better we know the past, the better we will understand ourselves. But that is a merely utilitarian

28

consideration. There is another, more important way in which the Church is a living vine through time.

This truth springs from the words, 'I am the vine, you are the branches'. The vine is Christ. He is really present in his Church, and this has been true in every age. The real presence of Christ in the first-century Church, the eighth-century, the fourteenth-century, the nineteenth-century Church. His presence is there, as promised. That is something before which to kneel. His voice speaks to us from the past in unique, never to be repeated ways, and to it we have to listen. Christ is one, and his Church is one, in space, in time and beyond, into the eternal. It is because Christ is present and alive in our past, that we have to listen to him there, conscious that we are here for but a short season, and then we have to hand on to the future generation those things which keep the Church in Christ. Our role is the awesome one of stewards; and it is precisely because Christ is the one we must listen to in the Church's history, that we cannot merely cook up slavish imitations of former ages. Past times can never be repeated. They have gone from our sight. But at their heart is the living sap, that unbroken life of Christ coursing through the vine of his Church. We can never repeat the past. Our task is to unlock those things in it which will enable us to build a living future.

But we must watch our language. We are the branches, not the vinedresser. Christ will work in us, 'so that we will bring out of our treasure what is new and what is old'. We do not work alone.

If we despise history, the ironical result is that we become imprisoned in our own time, and cannot see beyond it.

> What we call the beginning is often the end
> And to make an end is to make a beginning.
> The end is where we start from ...
>
> We are born with the dead:
> See, they return, and bring us with them ...
>
> A people without history
> is not redeemed from time, for history is a pattern
> of timeless moments.[21]

Christ comes from the past, from below the bedrock of our ancient memories, growing, ever on and on, the eternal and unfailing vine, through all the centuries, through, through to this vital moment, when he presents us with a living inheritance which is the seed of the future.

This is not merely held out to us; it is within us, for we are the branches of the vine, which is Christ. When, therefore, I pray alone, or when I attend the Eucharist or light a candle in church or make the sign of the cross, it is not a new act suddenly exploding on the world: it is put into my hands by the Body of Christ, which transcends time. When the community stages its worship on Sunday, it has to be careful to be sensitive to what is given us by the vine. There will be creativity, yes. There will even be some things which are novelties, yes. But they must grow out of the vine. The Church's worship evolves as it goes along. But it is always evolution, never revolution. It always preserves a sustained reverence for the vine, so that all new growth may shoot from it. Sometimes the Church is in danger of being several plants: a vine all tangled up with a Virginia creeper and a convolvulus.

Often it is even worse. It seems to believe that God works by spontaneous combustion. Here is the book (the Bible), here are the principles (doctrine), here are the structures (clergy and administration). Transplant them anywhere, and hey, presto! You can have the 'Christian faith', capable of popping up anywhere without relation to anything else. We take a small part of the Church's inheritance and treat it like a beer-making kit or a kit for making your own garage. Anyone can pick up the stuff, take it away and set it up where they like. This is typical of smaller Christian sects, but even the mainstream Churches frequently see things this way. Perhaps we see it in the General Synod of the Church of England, at times when it seems to legislate away as if it were the one Church of Christ, oblivious of all other Christians. This is a not infrequent complaint heard, for instance, from our Methodist friends.

The same goes for much theological reflection whether in universities or in parishes, whether it be lectures or discussion groups, where the 'gospel' can be talked about as if the only point of reference were the Bible, without any sense of the context of the wider Church in space and time.

It is seen yet again in that peculiar Anglican foible, the Anglican cycle of prayer, which leads us to pray as if the rest of the Church didn't exist. All of this is the religion of the beer-making kit. Then we have to start scratching our heads to work out why the beer has no fizz, or the garage is too small for the car. We have developed a blind spot for continuity, we cannot see the full consequences of being branches of the vine.

This problem arises not only when we ignore important parts of the vine. It happens when we start adding bits too. We have tried to show that we have a constitutional need to have 'card games' to play with God. But we asked 'Will *any* game do?' The answer clearly is No. Some things pass the test, some don't. Scripture clearly does. So do icons, church buildings and the Peace, for instance. They are clearly vine. In Songs of Praise, Derbyshire well-dressing and even Christian yoga there are usually sufficient connections to be seen. The same cannot be said of playing whist, knitting or pony-breeding. There are also borderline cases, such as some church social activities, or bell-ringing, or cleaning the church brass, or even some church choirs. This is not to deny that knitting or bell-ringing cannot be wholesome and wholly praise-worthy. Nor is it to say that Christ cannot be present in them. But it is to distinguish them from 'kits' whose special and avowed aim and gift is that they are ways of theological commerce with God, in which he and we explicitly aim to encounter each other. We may well be able to meditate while knitting, but that is almost incidental. To make a religious ceremony out of knitting or horse-breeding would be so far-fetched as to be ludicrous.

The point of clarifying this distinction is that many aspects of church life which we have inherited do often receive today this very accusation of being far-fetched or ludicrous, and often this is simply because we have lost sight of the vine which bears them. On the other hand we can end up doing other things in church which seem fine to us, but seem ludicrous or inappropriate to anyone who takes seriously the vine.

An example from parish life would be clerical behaviour. We have properly reacted against much stuffiness and formality in our immediate past. But we are deeply wounded by the thought that it has driven people away. We are a wounded Church because people have deserted us in their droves. We are therefore raw and hypersensitive in this area and often make the mistake of over-compensating. So a minister can dress in church as if his dress didn't really matter. He can walk and look around as if his bearing didn't matter. A minister can make frequent jokes and asides (rather than judicious rare ones) as if worship has to be as close to everyday life as possible. For, he or she may say, to attempt dignity and formality on a housing estate is far-fetched. Or to treat the sanctuary area with reverence is ludicrous with a God who bids us call him 'Abba'.

There is a lot of truth in this. But often there is an error in not appreciating the very fine balance that has to be struck, always different for every community and every place. The practices which we think are 'stuffy' may in reality bear with them a fertile and life-giving hinterland. Each may be a lid to God's Aladdin's cave. We should take great care before we concrete them over.

*Any* game in church will not do. Particularly when it is new, it needs to be tested rigorously before it can with reasonable certainty be recognized as a new bud on the vine. If it is, then it will become, not this congregation's bright idea, that priest's foible, but the Church at prayer. The mood, the style, the 'feel' of worship are either ecclesial (of the Church) or they are not. You can tell it straight away. Sometimes we plainly know that in this act of worship the Church of past, present and future is standing in the presence of God, and bringing with it the world and all its needs. It can be in a cathedral (but by no means always), a country church, a monastery, prayer in a city youth club, the Salvation Army on a street corner. But sometimes it is all too plain that the vine is the other side of a brick wall, the Church of past, present and future are specks on the horizon, and God's people are left to fumble with baubles of passing worth.

By now the reader may be thinking: 'All you are doing is trying to peddle tradition at the expense of renewal, and romantic make-believe in place of common sense.' That is indeed exactly what it looks like, and for this reason it is now necessary to turn our attention to that apparently rock-like but essentially quick and lively word, 'tradition'.

# CHAPTER 4 *The Tradition*

The word 'tradition' has many uses. It can, for instance, refer to practices that have got stuck, but which have certain virtues in their stuckness. Like the changing of the guard at Buckingham Palace, they may be expressive of the value we put on certain institutions, and the pride we have in them. Often such traditions are peculiar and odd, and their very oddity makes them a perfect vehicle for expressing the uniqueness of an institution. In the royal procession at the opening of Parliament each year we see men walking in reverse in order not to turn their back on the monarch, and a personage who carries a vertical pole on top of which is perched what looks like a nightcap. It seems to be part of the British bent for irony to take a particular delight in such things.

The Church too has many traditions such as these. They are 'traditions' in the *plural*, many of them playing a positive role in church life, but being, when the worst comes to the worst, expendable. As judges and barristers remove their wigs in heat waves, so there are times when Christians dispose of such 'traditions': on the battlefield, for example, or in the sick-room, or when in prison, when use of candles, vestments, altar, singing, and other things may be either impractical or unavailable.

Some of these traditions are more important than others. Some are so important symbolically that we only manage without them when in extreme circumstances. But traditions in the plural, important as many of them are, are not to be confused with 'Tradition' in the *singular*. Traditions are there because they are there. Tradition is there because it is alive. When traditions are rooted in this 'Tradition' they too become alive, being infected with its life. So a church building has an altar not merely through custom, nor for practicality, but because of the importance accorded it by the Tradition.

The Latin *traditio* means 'handing-on', something passed from hand to hand like the baton in a relay race. But it is more than that, it develops as it goes. A good example of tradition is a local accent. Different localities, particularly in European countries, have their own pronunciation. In Britain this can vary from town to town. Local pronunciation illustrates well the fact that tradition is extraordinarily tough. It can take a lot of battering. It was thought at one time that the introduction of radio and television would see the end of local accents, leading to a standard pronunciation. This may be the eventual result, but on present showing it is going to take a long time.

The English language itself is an admirable example of tradition. It has roots going back through human history into the dimmest distance of the earliest stirrings of civilization, and bears marks of every stage between then and now, the layers building up in an enormous compost heap. Part of its very richness lies in being able to bring into play different layers of that particular compost heap which is British and European cultural history. This hinterland is constantly drawn on in phrases like: 'on the nail', 'winter of discontent', 'a rum do', 'going to the wall', 'up a gum tree', 'hocus pocus', 'a rose by any other name', and thousands more, one very good reason why attempts to create new languages such as Esperanto have to fail. How could such a compost heap simply be created by the careful thought of a few?

It is in this kind of way that the Tradition of the Church needs to be understood: as a living, growing compost heap. Or, if we were to compare it with, say, a bush, we could say that 'traditions' are merely the woody branches; the 'Tradition', however, is the sap and the green leaves and blossom. Without that, 'traditions' turn to dead wood; with it, they become a living part of its vocabulary.

It is often pointed out that the Church has had such a turbulent history with so many interruptions, disasters and loss of heritage, that to speak of its Tradition in this way smacks of make-believe. For instance, it could be said that the monastic tradition was so thoroughly extirpated in Britain at the Reformation that its recent revival can claim no direct inheritance of Tradition.

There are several things to be said in response to this very reasonable objection. First of all, survival of *practices* through sheer habit is something deeply ingrained in the constitution of human society. Various authors, for instance, have unearthed abundant evidence of the survival of all sorts of medieval practices in the Church of England until the nineteenth century, such as

34

genuflecting to the altar, the sign of the cross, holy wells, prayer to saints, use of vestments, incense, the Angelus bell, and many other things.[22]

A second phenomenon is the persistence of *attitudes*. To take a secular example, English people can be so incorrigibly English. What on earth is a Frenchman or a Mongolian, for instance, to make of a lot of British humour? Two men are at a bus stop; it is teeming with rain, pouring cats and dogs, a veritable monsoon, sheets of water. The Englishman leans over to the startled foreign tourist, and confides between his teeth with a controlled smile: 'a bit damp'. The foreigner stares in disbelief, and begins to gesticulate. 'Damp? Damp? It's soaking wet, I'm drenched to the skin. What does he mean—damp?' The Englishman had assumed too much—so much as not to see the extent of his very Englishness. Somerset Maugham once said that you need to have lived in at least two foreign countries in order to understand your own. The particular cast of our thought, our sense of humour, our morality, our tastes and preferences, our cuisine and much more, reflect a tradition which is of great antiquity, and, for all that it changes as it goes along, is as deep-rooted as the marrow of our bones, and as tough as leather.

Tradition of this kind is ingrained and pervasive to an extent that we totally underestimate. Unless we are the kind of blinkered tourist that is not in short supply in Anglo-Saxon countries, it is something which can knock us for six when we go abroad.

I was once sitting in a village café somewhere in the middle of France, revelling in the particularity of it all, when I was vouch-safed a vision of how radically different it was from, say, Watford or Wigan. A delivery man stood up to depart and proceeded first to do up the belt of his overall. The performance was stunning. Standing erect with the poise of a Fred Astaire, by deft and accomplished hand movements he threaded the belt's end through the buckle and with consummate panache drew it out before him in a graceful flourish, to get exactly the right tightness, then deftly completed the operation and strode out through the door to his float like Olivier to Agincourt. English people have to go to drama school to learn the secret of *présence*, but the French are born with it. It is part of their ancient tradition, and would take more than an avalanche of revolutions to rub it out of them. And just as other peoples act differently from us, so they think differently too.

Once, when driving over the border into Italy, I was told I had to go to Milan for the papers I needed. So I went there. An official showed me into his dark office with a grand, kingly bearing worthy of Caesar Augustus or one of the Medici. 'This is my office', he seemed to say, in a quite harmless and innocent manner, 'and I am *very important*, and am holding court.' In order to get my papers, I would need at least to play up to this game, and put on the manners of a courtier seeking favours. Unfortunately for both of us, I came from a different country and a different tradition, and didn't have it in me, and would jolly well sooner burn anyway. So I behave as if I were in Watford. The official's grandiloquence and ingratiating smile disappear suddenly, like little Willy, who finds that little Johnny doesn't want to play. I should have got the papers at the border. He can't provide them. I wonder, totally unworthily, if now he wants a bribe. Fatal. Not in a thousand years am I going to pay something which is not meant to be paid. Now I am Disgusted, Tunbridge Wells. I'm not going till I've got my papers. This is a free country, the law's the law ... He looks at me in disbelief, convinced I'm a rogue or a madman. After a protracted siege the man ultimately throws some papers at me. They turn out later to have fatal errors in them but it doesn't matter, for Italy is such a human and humorous country that no one ever inspects them. Here was a meeting between two ancient traditions, each with its virtues, each with its drawbacks. I held no grudge for long, for I was soon to have a meal, and, as is so rightly said about eating in Italy, you sit at the table with a sense of being human beings to your fingertips, but rise feeling like gods. I hope I have since learned not to be quite so bone-headed about what are purely English values. Italy and Britain are very different—*vive la différence!*

Our Traditions are ancient and ingrained. They make us what we are to an extent that would astonish us if we could see it. Wars, revolutions, mass movements of population, plague, famine and all the disasters under the sun can leave Tradition's essential continuity intact. A Tradition is a style, a 'touch', a feel, a vocabulary of attitudes and preferences, an inimitable something born of accumulated experience and interaction, and so close to us that for much of the time we cannot see it.

We go about unaware that we are ineluctably part of a tradition. Look even at the distinct differences in character between Welsh people, English, and Scots, and Irish, and even between Yorkshire and Lancashire folk. All of these are traditions which go far back in history.

If we now turn to the Church, we find just the same phenomenon. The Christian Tradition is so tough that it can even seem to disappear but then come back. We can find remarkable examples of the capacity of Tradition to lie dormant for long periods without dying. In eighteenth-century Transylvania the Habsburg occupiers determined to convert all Orthodox to the Roman obedience, and, knowing that monasteries played a key role in Orthodox life, they had them all destroyed. The ordinary people who flocked to monasteries on Sundays and festivals, and saw them as the heart of their Christian life, were left with nothing. So in every peasant home there arose a little 'monastery', a part of the house crammed with crude icons painted on glass, which the family would 'visit' at the times when they used to visit the monastery. For two hundred years they kept the memory of the monastery alive, until eventually their monasteries were restored to them. Anyone who has seen the riches of Orthodox monasticism in Transylvania and the vigorous part it plays in the life of the Church cannot but be impressed at the enduring powers of Tradition. For monastic life depends on a sufficient foundation of understanding in its local church, not least if it is to draw any recruits.

Recovery of lost traditions is something found also in the arts. It might be thought that particular ways of performing music, once lost, would be irrecoverable. But where there is sufficient documentary material, and where contemporary tradition has not moved on so far as to be fatally foreign, a tradition can spring from hibernation into new life. Francis Kline gives an example from opera, in the recovery of the lost art of *Bel Canto* by Maria Callas in the 1950s:

> Though the demands of Bel Canto technique and the passion to communicate music through them were observable from the score of Donizetti, Bellini and others, and though a conductor of the stature of Serafin could conceive intellectually what the music should sound like, it would take a singer who could enter the ethos of the era of Bel Canto, intuit its development and supply the incredible effort to mold her voice, her personality and her artistic expression into the contours of its technique in order to bring Bel Canto opera alive. This Callas did repeatedly. One can hear from recording to magical recording the rediscovery of the secrets of Bel Canto in this one singer alone. What

37

exercises she practised to shape her voice, what formulae she abstracted from those scores and repeated over and over until perfection was obtained is known only to Callas. For she was not a teacher. But it is a marvelous fact in the musical scene of the 50s, 60s and 70s that singers, spurred on by the Callas example, kept knocking at the door of Bel Canto, until they plundered its storerooms of many of its treasures. Much of that repertoire has since come again to the light, and thanks to Callas, Sutherland, Sills and others, the technique of Bel Canto has been reconstructed in a way much more conscious and analytical than when it was first developed. Whether or not Bel Canto has ever lived in our times as it once did in the eighteenth century is open to question. What must be said about its rediscovery, though, is the evident joy of creation, gift and discovery as the Callas voice ripples dramatically through bravura passages with a feeling and musical sense that reveal the Bel Canto repertoire as the great music it is. Here we may observe the technique of Bel Canto and the obvious dependence of otherwise dead musical scores on a tradition of enlightened performance technique.[23]

We have no way of proving that this tradition has been resurrected exactly as it was, but at least one way of testing it is by its fruits: if the music becomes greater music than it was before, then it must be that something of the spirit of its tradition has been touched upon.

Perhaps even more remarkable is the story of the restoration of the religious life in the Church of England. Everything appeared to have been swept away in the middle of the sixteenth century. After so many centuries, how could the once fertile compost heap of the English monastic tradition ever be recovered? The revival, from the 1840s onwards, proved, however, to be extraordinarily successful. It could never have been done, say, in the Calvinist Church of Scotland. Nor could it have been done on such a scale in other parts of the Anglican world, where the necessary environment of understanding was lacking, in British India, say, or other parts under British governance and cultural influence, such as what is now Nigeria. Monasticism depends on having an environment where there is at least some minimal understanding and sympathy in the population. Monasticism can only take hold where it resonates with the local Church. There was something about the culture and the setting of Victorian England, and the disposition of the population, which made a monastic revival so possible, even though the difficulties were, and continue to be, enormous.

Part of the answer lies in the extent to which we were formed by our medieval past, and the way this determined the nature of the Anglican Reform. Of all countries before the Reformation, England was one of the most monastic. It was a Church, for instance, which had monastic cathedrals, a rare phenomenon in Christian history. After the Reformation, the monastic tradition was fragmented into debris, but these pieces of debris went on in their own corners, living and partly living. In the colleges of the universities a retired, studious life was being lived around court-yards and cloisters. College fellows had to be celibate, so there was nothing new even there. When religious communities started to live a similar kind of life, their daily office would have been no oddity, for people were familiar with it, in cathedral, college and parish. The very choir stalls in which they sat would be no innovation, and redolent indeed of the 'Benedictine' studiousness of cathedral canons, and the retired life of the cathedral close. Together with cells, refectories, dormitories, and other things less easy to define, but taking the form of inherited attitudes and sympathies, this could be referred to as the 'indigenous debris' of the monastic tradition.

There are, however, other sources for recovery of the tradition which transcend national boundaries. Perhaps these could be called 'international debris'. For instance, protagonists of the Anglican monastic revival visited continental communities in order to imbibe all they could of the wisdom and old-fashioned know-how which is part of the stuff of living tradition. It is interesting to see that, because they were content to limit such visits mainly to France, the revival in some ways took on a pronounced French stamp. Had they gone further afield they would have recovered an even broader vision.

In any project to restore an aspect of living Tradition, all of these things can play an important role. But there is one more dimension yet to be added to the project and that is the very important role to be played by the literature of the Tradition. Monastic life on the continent has also known its interruptions, such as the havoc wrought by Napoleon. A vital part in its restoration has been played by matching the debris with the literature. There is a vast accumulation of writings on the religious life from the earliest centuries down to the present day, and the assiduity with which since the seventeenth and eighteenth centuries religious com-munities have ordered and edited this literature and engaged in the study of it must be reckoned a crucial factor in making the survival of the monastic tradition possible.

This subject is unfamiliar to many, but it shows particularly clearly how versatile, tough and enduring Tradition proves often to be. It can lie dormant in sublimated forms for long periods, later to be fanned into flame again by a combination of intuition, cross-fertilization of debris, and recourse to the memory bank of its literary inheritance.

This becomes doubly clear when we compare the revival of the religious life with other parts of Tradition which have truly died. Although the monarchy in Britain seems to flourish abundantly, restoration of the same in France would be inconceivable. The Sarum liturgy of medieval England may undergo occasional attempts at revival, but they have too little to build on, and must remain lifeless.

Perhaps now we can begin to see what we might mean in talking about Tradition in the Church. For all that it might seem invisible and vacuous, it is far more tough and vigorous than we can always see from our standpoint within it. It is also confusingly manifold. Here is no monumental block of codified lore. Rather is it like the model of a DNA molecule, infuriatingly complex and many-faceted, and changing slowly as it goes along. Tradition can never be stuck. Once it is stuck it ceases to be Tradition and becomes a museum-piece. No, it presses forward, and we are its 'business end'. The Tradition hands on to us building blocks with which we are to build the future in our own style. The Tradition is like a language, in one sense. You may speak the English language in a boring and pedantic way; or you may speak it in a lively and imaginative way. What you cannot do is coin too many words at once. That way the discourse collapses, the continuing chain-reaction is interrupted, and you end up saying nothing, because no one will understand you.

In case the Tradition of the Church may still seem to have too many cloud-like properties, it would be helpful here to attempt a sketch of what principally goes to make it up. What *is* this so-called Tradition? Is it any more than mere frames of mind? No, it is very concrete. It is the Church, the Body of Christ, and the order which constitutes her, principally the priesthood of the baptized and the prime forms of service of bishop, presbyter and deacon. It is the Holy Spirit, who is her life-breath. It is the faith as handed on down the centuries, and enshrined in the Holy Scriptures which were formed both with and by the Tradition. It is fed by the teachings of the Fathers of the Church and their interpretation of the Scriptures, and it is the faith as acted out and lived by saints and sinners down the ages. Central to it are the call to service, the call to mission, and the call to spend and be spent for our neighbour and for the world, to be ministers of forgiveness, and embodiments of love. The Tradition is the Eucharist on the Lord's day, the hours of prayer of the divine office, the calendar, the sacraments and sacramentals, the art and symbolism of the Church, and all her attendant paraphernalia. Obviously, even a simple sketch could fill a fat tome.

The Tradition is a vocabulary. Without it we cannot speak. It is like language to your baby. As he learns to speak so he is enabled to engage with life. Those who are unfortunate enough not to be able to learn to speak have to follow what is the vocation of a few: to depend on those who can speak. What we speak is simply a language. It may be English, French or Swahili. There is no great mystique about it. It simply does its job, enabling us to engage with life. What we mean here about the Tradition is precisely this: it puts into our hands a kit of tools, a vocabulary. This vocabulary, like a language such as English, has a richness, a depth and an experience to it that cannot be invented on the spot. To try and create a Tradition out of nothing is to concoct a kind of ecclesiastical Esperanto.

We don't, however, keep a self-conscious eye on the riches and the depths every waking moment; we get on with the job of practical living. For those who have some experience of computers, the program is a good illustration of the function of the Tradition. Without it no task can be done on the computer. But once the program is in place, we turn our direct attention from it, and get on with our task.

If we return to our list of things which make up the Tradition (baptism, ordination, Eucharist, Bible, etc.) we can see that something very simple is being asked of us: to treat these things with the appropriate degree of seriousness, to accord to them the worth which is their due, and then watch how everything changes. They are treated with *reverence*, and not simply as material objects to be manipulated at will. The reverence is not for them in themselves, but for the Love of which they are the expression.

The other side of that coin is that it belongs to reverence to allow that which is revered to live and to change. You may greatly value a beautiful bush in your garden, but you have to accept it will continue to grow, perhaps into something which is not so beautiful to you. You can only stop it growing by killing it. Here we have not a superstitious reverence which blocks the Tradition's life, but something like the reverence of the sculptor for the wood which already contains the shape he is to draw out of it. The Christian Tradition, if you like, is a Mighty Wurlitzer. We inherit it, play our own tunes on it, add a few stops here and there, and then hand it forward to others.

It is, finally, a part of the Tradition's very growth and development that we apply to it those critical faculties given us by God for courageous testing of all truth. The Tradition invites our biting blows; indeed it deserves them for its own integrity and ours. However, as we shall see, this needs a slightly more refined approach than that of the bull in the china shop.

We are speaking about something which is the very life of the Church, the Holy Spirit blowing through her. The Tradition cannot exist without the living community of the Church, and it cannot live if it ever stands still. Since the word 'tradition' as used today can be so misleading through our misuse of it, it may be better to use some other word, such as 'the Momentum'. Here is something of a different order from mere conservatism. It is the momentum of the life of the community. We are a people in momentum, propelled by the lively dance of the Holy Spirit.

There are some places where a vision based on this Momentum of the Church may seem too unrealistic. An obvious example would be some inner city parishes. It might seem obvious there that a new tradition needs to be created for a new world. The problem is that Tradition is an irreplaceable language. Imagine the success of any government which sought to abolish English and replace it with a new language invented to meet modern needs. Any such project would be totally unrealistic.

There is, however, perhaps another possibility which is not too far from this. In a Church which is in healthy contact with its Momentum, and which understands itself after the manner outlined in this book, there will perhaps be room for significant departures here and there. To take a monastic example, it is not unheard-of for a religious community to have one member who is a bit of a maverick, who seems to live in a way which is eccentric or at least significantly different. A monastery can often bear having

42

one person like that, or perhaps a couple, if the total community is strong in faithfulness to its way. It can bear such a thing, but only if it is publicly acknowledged and publicly agreed, so that all is honestly shared. In a case of mere collusion, however, or of turning a blind eye, it can then have great power for ill.

Similarly, in a Church which holds well to the things it should hold on to, there may well be room for departures of more than the usual adventurousness in places where the need for such is very great. But it all depends on the lines of communication flowing, attitudes of mutual reverence being sound and well. Then, for instance, a normal parish may benefit from contact with a way-out inner-city parish, and vice versa, and the one indeed will need the other. But the Church can only bear so much departure from structures which, it is to be hoped, will be pretty flexible anyway for life in a society such as ours.

Our problem is that we easily slide back into thinking of the Tradition as some abstract will-o'-the-wisp. We need to be called back regularly to the fact that it is the concrete furniture of the Church first and foremost, and that its function is very practical and down-to-earth. It is like the painter's palette. No palette, no painting: just a scratchy outline.

A final question might be raised here. If the Tradition is so important, why is it that so many new things are being said about it? Why can we find little of this elucidation of the Tradition in the writings of former ages? Here we find a further insight into our situation. Both within and outside Christianity, a phenomenon is taking place which is largely new in the evolution of civilization. Our age is sometimes called the age of analysis, and we see taking place in many areas of human life an analysing and codifying of things which until now have been taken for granted. We can see it all around us, in psychology, marriage guidance, music-making, church building, the sociology of the city, and so on. Life is being analysed and reflected upon, and often this involves the revival or recovery of things which were on the verge of disappearing. Ecology, art restoration techniques and even the renewed craft of thatching roofs, have come into view hardly a moment too soon. Sometimes the result is simple conservation; but sometimes too it means taking up a living tradition again and developing it further.

In a similar manner in the Church we analyse and codify, recovering from present practice and past history things which surprise and enlighten us, and we pick them up, consolidate them, and take them further. That is certainly true, for example, of the liturgical renewal which we have seen over the last twenty-five years.

In one way this means traditions have changed for ever, because until now their pursuit was largely unreflective; once they have been dissected and evaluated, however, the whole enterprise will inevitably be more self-conscious. This is a process which can only strengthen and consolidate them for the future, and all the signs are that the time is ripe for the Church's Tradition to begin to receive the same treatment.

In the light of all this we are now able to look back and say that if the Church needs 'card games', rigmaroles, forms of symbol and action, if it is to have depth to its life; and if people need a 'kit' of such things in order to be Christian, one of the first places we should look for all this will be the Church's Tradition: largely a host of phenomena, material and conceptual, rolling forward and changing as they go in the momentum of the Spirit, but in need today of much more careful and systematic assessment than they have received in the immediate past.

# CHAPTER 5 *Community*

Many British people have the very curious belief that when eating with a knife and fork the food has to be perched on the curved hump of the fork's back, where it is likely to fall off, rather than nestling naturally in the hollow of the fork's other side. This is a source of frequent comment by foreigners, who cannot understand why great contortions and balancing acts should be endured for the simple purpose of eating peas, or scooping up last morsels. This is a rather obvious example of the way our behaviour, our thoughts, our attitudes, are very rarely our own, but have mostly been programmed into us by our context, which in this case is British society (of a certain kind). I have written elsewhere on this subject[24] and will not repeat myself here, except to say that the British foible of the reversed fork is simply a more outstanding example of the way in which our personalities have been profoundly determined by the context which has produced us. This British context gave us birth, has nurtured us and inculcated our attitudes and manners from the cradle, and we can be nothing but its products.

However, if the context changes, we change. If I move from being a country vicar to being a prison chaplain different issues will come to the forefront of my mind, and things which loom largest in my life and have a greater vividness will be different from those which were so in the country parish. I will see the world differently.

More than that, our world structures our sense of ourselves. A successful tycoon whose business collapses will be seen to be a shadow of himself. He will cease to walk like a powerful man, his forcefulness in gesture and expression may even be seen to falter. This is why it is no joke at all to be among the ranks of the long-term unemployed. The detrimental effects on one's state of mind can even be felt physically by the person involved. We depend on our context for our sense of ourselves. When it is taken away, we change.

45

The Vicar of Bray regularly changed his politics according to the nature of the regime in power. This might be called opportunism. But when it happens with whole nations we can see something else at work. In the English Reformation there was strong initial resistance to the religious changes. But a point was reached when the consensus became so strong that adherence to the old religion began to carry with it an increasing sense of unreality, except for a few stalwarts endowed with exceptional courage and singlemindedness. Whatever prevails bestows reality. Consensuses can sometimes collapse or melt away, such as at the end of the Commonwealth in 1660, or the collapse of the colonels' regime in Greece, when the cabinet suddenly realized one morning that it was utterly unreal to continue meeting, and all closed their briefcases and went home. When such a regime has gone, people can find it difficult to understand why they were so resigned to it before, and even be surprised at how they came to be convinced by its rhetoric. The prevailing consensus and ethos profoundly determine how we live and think.

We know similar shifts in our own experience. In the 1950s it would have been unthinkable for footballers to embrace. By the 1970s that had almost become part of the job description.

Something which is particularly interesting for us is how this phenomenon operates in the realm of ideas and attitudes. For instance, faith healers in Italy tend to cause traffic jams and chaos. In Britain, few people show any interest on that scale. In fourth-century Constantinople theology was the most serious and 'real' item in the news. In the modern West it is perhaps economics. In certain parts of the USA, life seems to be all play. In Victorian England, the golden standard was work. Any of these values would be unthinkable, 'unreal', if transferred from one to another of these contexts.

At certain times and in certain places certain things are possible to believe and others are not. Or they can only be believed with the aid of special effort and forms of extra support. Christian belief, too, varies in detail and emphasis from place to place and between one time and another. For most people the only tenable form of belief is that which roughly corresponds to the prevailing form. So in our own age it becomes easy to believe in Christian service, in informality, in the Church's prophetic role, in full participation by all in the liturgy. But it becomes difficult to believe in the resurrection, the inspiration of Scripture, in reverence, and in the Tradition.

A fact of stunning importance emerges from this: for all our exaggerated modern emphasis on the individual and his or her 'personal' faith, this proves to be a mirage. The only faith which turns out to be 'real' and possible is faith which is compatible with the society in which we are set. There are many variations and apparent (but far from real) exceptions, but this is the overwhelming general situation. However much we may wish it to be otherwise, the faith is exercised by the community, and only by derivation does the individual hold on to it. Our attitudes are typical of our age. It is from there that they take their origin and their sense of reality, rather than simply from our 'inner self'.

If this is so, we are faced with two serious problems. First, there is the problem of being able to describe more fully what it means in down-to-earth terms to speak of the faith being held by the community for the individual. The second problem is more serious, however, and therefore needs to be tackled first. It is the very obvious fact that we live in a pluralist society, and the Church herself is pluralist, embracing within her bounds wide varieties of belief and practice. This seems to compromise what we have said about the power of context to confer a sense of reality, and also seriously questions any possibility of the Church ever adhering unanimously to the Tradition. The Tradition is simply one contending voice among many. This fact lies at the heart of the argument of a book which may well prove to have marked a watershed in the career of the cluster of issues we have so far examined.

Alasdair MacIntyre's *After Virtue*[25] seeks to show how, beginning from the seventeenth century, Western civilization gradually came to lose touch with its Tradition. One of the effects of this has been the loss of a common basis for holding a discussion on a wide range of matters. There results a shortage of real argument in modern debate. One politician insists that each person has a right to what he or she has earned. Another politician insists that all people deserve equal provision. The arguments are incommensurate, like trying to say how many pears are worth an orange. The arguments shoot past each other. Neither can win, neither can lose, on the basis of argument alone. The result is that the winner becomes the one who shouts loudest.

We find the same phenomenon time and again, wherever we look. A public inquiry into the building of a motorway will hear *ad nauseam* of the relative merits of easing the traffic burden or saving a rare natural habitat. Only the most vocal can win, the party which puts on the most pressure, stages the most effective demonstration; for there is no common ground on which a solution can be arrived at by the exercise of pure reason.

One result of this is that indignation is a peculiarly modern stance, says MacIntyre. This inability to hold a true argument for want of a common ground pervades the whole of our life: commerce, the law courts, the shop, the factory, the Church, the family, and even religious communities. There are few shared criteria left, and on most matters we plump for this or that point of view largely out of personal preference. The terrible disillusionment is the discovery that, contrary to hopes, founding a world on pure reason does not work. Reason today is impotent to conclude a vast range of arguments.

Even those who disagree with MacIntyre's general thesis accept this as ineluctable fact. We pay lip service to reason, yet fail to acknowledge the extent to which it has failed in its promise to produce a perfectly ordered world. The gap left by it has been filled by a strange substitute: personal preference. This is held to be the most natural, commonsense, taken-for-granted basis for individual belief and attitudes. One term used to describe this position is *emotivism*. MacIntyre describes emotivism as meaning that all evaluative judgements are merely expressions of preference, attitude or feeling.[26]

Were emotivism to sweep all before it then our society would descend into chaos. But in practice it is held in with some rather flimsy fencing. This is made up of unacknowledged and unrecognized debris of the shattered Tradition.

In order to illustrate what has happened to the Tradition in Western society MacIntyre tells a parable about something which is a good example of a living tradition: science. Science is always conscious of its evolution and of its antecedents, and its more recent history. But it is also constantly innovative, moving forward from what has been established to what is to follow. In itself science is a good example of Tradition. But MacIntyre's parable upon it shows what can go wrong:

Imagine that the natural sciences were to suffer the effects of a catastrophe. A series of environmental disasters are blamed by the general public on the scientists. Widespread riots occur, laboratories are burnt down, physicists are lynched, books and instruments are destroyed. Finally a Know-Nothing political movement takes power and successfully abolishes science teaching in schools and universities, imprisoning and executing the remaining scientists. Later still there is a reaction against this destructive movement and enlightened people seek to revive science, although they have largely forgotten what it was. But all that they possess are fragments: a knowledge of experiments detached from any knowledge of the theoretical context which gave them significance; parts of theories unrelated either to the other bits and pieces of theory which they possess or to experiment; instruments whose use has been forgotten; half-chapters from books, single pages from articles, not always fully legible because torn and charred. None the less all these fragments are re-embodied in a set of practices which go under the revived names of physics, chemistry and biology. Adults argue with each other about the respective merits of relativity theory, evolutionary theory and phlogiston theory, although they possess only a very partial knowledge of each. Children learn by heart the surviving portions of the periodic table and recite as incantations some of the theorems of Euclid. Nobody, or almost nobody, realises that what they are doing is not natural science in any proper sense at all. For everything that they do and say conforms to certain canons of consistency and coherence and those contexts which would be needed to make sense of what they are doing have been lost, perhaps irretrievably.

In such a culture men would use expressions such as 'neutrino', 'mass', 'specific gravity', 'atomic weight' in systematic and often interrelated ways which would resemble in lesser or greater degrees the ways in which such expressions had been used in earlier times before scientific knowledge had been so largely lost. But many of the beliefs presupposed by the use of these expressions would have been lost and there would appear to be an element of arbitrariness and even of choice in their application which would appear very surprising to us. What would appear to be rival and competing premises for which no further argument could be given would abound. Subjectivist theories of science would appear and would be criticised by those who held that the notion of truth embodied in what they took to be science was incompatible with subjectivism.

This imaginary possible world is very like one that some science fiction writers have constructed. We may describe it as a world in which the language of natural science, or parts of it at least, continues to be used but is in a grave state of disorder.[27]

MacIntyre intends this as a parable of the state of morality in our society. Moral values in our society are an incoherent patchwork of debris.

Here, rather, we are concerned with the Church's Tradition, whose situation is not so disastrous, but yet close enough for MacIntyre's parable to be deeply haunting. This 'science' of the Tradition does survive in certain currents and certain communities in the Church, sufficient to be able to reconstruct or rediscover the whole. But these sources are frequently misunderstood or only half heeded.

The Church today is a chaos of contending voices, attempting in vain to conduct rational discussion, and failing to realize the extent to which the arguments pitted against each other are incommensurate. However, with the Church there is more hope, and the reason for that is that the Tradition survives in much bigger chunks. Scripture, liturgy, a sense of history, and, something which modern society lacks, some concept of a *telos*, a purpose and end to the journey. That purpose and end is love (far more satisfactory than 'rights' and personal preferences), love as found through the liturgy, in Christ and his relationship to the Father, and love as found in Christian service, love of our neighbour, and the calling, if necessary, to be a doormat. Our big problems lie in the areas where church life is most deeply fragmented.

In particular, we are plagued by too much theoretical head-stuff. For example, it is held to be important to be able to decide whether you can believe in Christ's resurrection. For if you can't, how do you celebrate Easter? Or it is thought to be important to refrain from forms of liturgy which express belief in something difficult to accept rationally, the Trinity, say, should you find it impossible to believe in it. The assumption behind this reasoning is that to follow Christ involves believing certain propositions are true.

Again we are back with St Benedict. Without the pre-existent monastic life and its compost heap of accumulated wisdom and certain matters of 'touch' which can only be handed on in community, his rule would be a dead letter. Crumbs from the table. So with propositions of the faith. As they stand they are neither here nor there. The Christian doctrine of the resurrection is to be found not in propositions but in the life of the Church, whose heart is her worship. If you have not already sniffed it there, then it matters not what propositions you manage to believe.

In the public forum, where every statement is mission in action, we shoot ourselves in the foot if we hold up such matters as the physical resurrection for intimate examination in public. The very proper honest questioning is secondary to the business of enabling people to hear God's music, to gain a whiff of the eternal worship of heaven. Then can come the honest inquiry, but let it keep its place. Those who make too much of a song and dance about it are playing straight into the hands of those they oppose. It is necessary to examine our beliefs rigorously, but normally that can only have any meaning within the household of the Church. To conduct debate on aspects of Christian doctrine in the public forum is like selling the story of your marriage to the Sunday papers—not likely to help the marriage.

Rigorous examination of doctrine needs to be carried out with precision, by the right people in the right places. And if you initiate questioning in the public arena, then you need to be able to express convincingly in the public arena what you *do* believe about the doctrine concerned. Success in this is very elusive. Such reconstructed doctrines nearly always come over as lame, for no one has yet been able to convey to the general public the wider context of the Church's life which enables doctrine to become more than flat, uninteresting abstractions; and in the process we lead people to believe that these mere abstractions are the total reality, whereas in fact, as we know, that reality is infinitely greater than these meagre words. Doctrine is mere shavings without the Church.

In addition it has to be said in all honesty that academic theologians often need closer experience of the parish. There is a kind of disillusionment which affects young clergy new from theological college as they discover what ordinary people and their thinking are really like. This experience is salutary and fruitful, but it can take many years of parish ministry for it fully to sink home, decades even. Until that lesson has been fully learned (if such a thing is possible) our mission, thinking and speaking are to a greater or lesser extent off beam. This particularly applies to launching of torpedoes against verbal formulations of the faith. Public examination of doctrine is a messy business, and may help some while damaging many others; and it generally takes the public's attention away from the front line where many Christians are struggling with more pressing realities.

Putting this another way, it can be said that Western Christianity has a fixation about *belief*. The Church's traditional fixation, however, is the person of the Father, whom we encounter through

Christ in the living hurly-burly of the Church's life. Modern people are not interested in the slightest in what theologians have to say about the physical resurrection, except perhaps out of that slight curiosity that can inform many a pub conversation. They are not, contrary to what is supposed, asking from their guts: 'What should I believe?' They are asking: 'Who is there? Whom may I meet and be saved? What must I *do*?' Head-stuff about belief comes later, and so is put in its rightful context.

Much 'theological' debate in periodicals and the media, and in theological colleges, is like the stranded dead leg of an animal which has gone we know not where. Much effort is made to relate this incomplete 'theology' to the contemporary world, when it is all ultimately impotent without proper integration into the momentum of the Church's Tradition. Training for ordination in the Church of England has in some places become fixated with what I have heard described as a 'patternism', a playing with patterns in an artificially created system of discourse. Typical is a document recently published on urban studies centres.[28] Such centres have bravely taken up the challenge to relate the gospel to the life of Urban Priority areas. But in this document we read over and over again about the quest for encounter with God in theological *studies*. 'Theology', as the authors understand it, is at the heart of students' formation. This 'theology' is a simple mould. The complex issues raised by the Momentum of the Church are narrowed down to this intellectual exercise. Just as children like green jelly not to be any old shape, but moulded into the shape of a rabbit, so we can always be tempted to light on one aspect of the manifold and slippery Christian project and put it on a grand plate at the centre of the table. Here this 'patternism' sets the pattern for everything. It becomes our controlling concept: 'theology'. This is understood to mean 'rigorous thought' about God and the world, rather than what theology truly is, a greater holistic whole which dances ungraspably like a flame.

Christian theology cannot be captured by the faculties of the head. We can't even *see* it if we try that. The only way to see it is in the entrails of the Church. Without that it becomes an all-too-earnest playing with patterns, out of touch with reality. Theology which is out of touch with reality is nothing new in the Church. Such 'theology' either tends to be too out of touch with real life (like a baroque ceiling painting) or, as in this case, too out of touch with the reality of the Church (then the faith appears like the flat, unconvincing characters in a bad novel).

The word 'theology' does not properly mean this exaggerated intellectualism. It refers to the whole life of the Church, whose controlling centre is, if anything, not these brain exercises but *theoria*, the beholding of God and the living out of its consequences (which will include rigorous academic inquiry as an essential element). This can only be pursued with any sense when understood as part of a greater whole, which will include such things as liturgy, prayer, exegesis, doctrine, ethics, and the pastoral and corporate life of the Church and her received traditions, in the continuity of her Momentum. Within such a scheme it has often been suspected that the liturgy has a privileged place.

Much of what passes for theology in the contemporary Church of England is Christian ratiocination as inherited from the Middle Ages. Then it was set in a rich and potent context. Now we continue the ratiocination not noticing that the context has melted away (except amongst the few whom it has kept a grip on). We are not calling for the Church to abandon this ratiocination, but to rediscover the context.

It often seems to be supposed that we worship because we believe. The Tradition, on the other hand, suggests that the Church believes because it worships. I remember very clearly an incident at school when I was about twelve. Music lessons were always fair game for misbehaviour. On this occasion, while the music master had his back to us as he put on a record, several of us stood and made what we thought were funny gestures. We aped the music, pulling faces and waving our arms about ridiculously. However, I was suddenly overwhelmed by a Beethoven symphony in a vivid and commanding flood, and sat down ashamed, rapt and riveted, overcome by a mystery and a majesty I had never known before. After that my conversion was total and I went on eventually to read music at university.

That is a parable of what is happening continually in the project of theology. It involves everyone, from professor to peasant. All are theologians. Criticism of modern 'theology' in the Church of England has an obligation to be trenchant, because we are faced here with a distortion which is smothering the Spirit. The curious fact about it is that, intended as a search for honesty and integrity, it turns out instead to be another way of having things on a plate. It is like a juggler reducing the number of balls he needs to keep in the air to one. And naturally we choose as the privileged ball one which puts everything in our grasp rather than God's.

To put it another way, it is right for us to discern that any faith which is worth its salt has to be a thinking, questioning, enquiring faith. But that cannot be its starting point. The starting point is a much more complex and manifold activity or state of being, which could be described as swimming in the Tradition. Which do we do first? Think or swim? To take thinking as your starting point is ultimately to sink. For it is to value the picture of the lion above the lion himself. It is to keep reason on a throne which it has irreversibly forfeited, as all thinking people have now to admit. Our reasoning faculties are vital to the Christian enterprise, but they cannot be allowed to be in the controlling position. Much ordination training today seems to be aimed primarily at equipping students to 'think theologically'. It all makes a sad tale in the light of the universal Christian calling to be caught up, heart, flesh and spirit in that 'love who moves the sun and the other stars'. Faith and hope are crowned by love, not by *talk* about love, or logic-chopping about it.

Head-stuff needs to be put in its proper place in relation to gut-stuff and grace-stuff. The result should be like the sportsman whose thinking, feeling, intuition, and physical and other powers are so integrated that he acts spontaneously and organically, without any need to exercise any of these faculties consciously—it all flows in a perfect unity. The modern Church has a grossly swollen brain. It is hooked on ratiocination based on an incoherent selection of fragments of a partly submerged Tradition. It has lost the knack of acting with the whole person. If, as we have suggested, faith, whatever its form, is always held by the community, and only derivatively by the individual, then we are stuck in a mess, an unresolvable cerebral squirm. Only one thing can be done to save the situation from eventual collapse, and that is to take up again the wholeness of the Tradition, and its integral understanding of the Christian way.

Here we are at last brought to look more closely at the first of the problems raised above, the idea that the primary location of faith is the Church.

A political party has within it many shades of opinion, and ultimately no two MPs will hold exactly the same views. But for the purposes of the party's effectiveness, MPs sink differences in the common cause, and will even make an effort to coach their own views towards being more commensurate with the common will. A political party might be thought an unedifying example, but the same thing can be found in any movement or society which espouses a certain cause or object, particularly where there are opponents to be challenged. This helps us to begin to gain a foothold in this modern Christian problem concerning belief. It can be said, again in rather disreputable terms, that it is in the interest of the gospel for us to be prepared where we possibly can to follow the 'party line' (as well as of challenging it when we are forced to). Put another way, this can be described as a generosity in some matters, due to reverence for the integrity of the overall project.

Clearly this is a poor argument on its own. But it is a start, and it has the virtue of showing that not only in the Church but also in the world commitment to a larger reality can take precedence over matters of individual detail.

Another obvious example would be the family. You have to be very careful what you say to anybody about members of their family. You have to be even more careful in a village, where networks of relationship can be all-pervasive. Blood runs thicker than water, even when relationships are distant. The possibility of being detached about being a Christian is surely at least as limited as detachment about being a mother or a son. Making light of such bonds proclaims for all to see that the bonds, if there at all, are tenuous. In many walks of life loyalty is seen as a virtue because those involved have come to the conclusion that on balance pursuit of the common goal will in the particular circumstances bring greater benefit than pursuit of individual goals.

Love for family in normal circumstances is valued higher than establishing public truth concerning its members (except, perhaps, in rare cases like murder or treason). If my sister does something very foolish through no fault of her own, but eventually comes to understand the nature of the mistake, I will not make of it a story for dinner parties or the pub. Just in the same way, the doctrine of the Church develops, so that what seems inspiring in one age can seem difficult in another. But there are ways of dealing with such things with love and tact, because the overall project is much greater, and by its side these questions are dwarfed. In many such family matters we settle for a deft and loving discretion. A naive way of expressing a doctrine can still be lifegiving, precisely because of the fact that it is a family matter. We shall be reluctant to pillory it in public.

In a similar way, there are many areas of human living where we have to be prepared to settle for what is given. The person looking for the perfect job will never get one. Many men today feel they deserve the perfect wife. The choice is either not to marry until she turns up, in which case they will wait for ever, or to feel free to change partners as and when necessary. This is not a male monopoly, of course. The realistic way (and hence the one that is likely to be our divine vocation) is to settle, ultimately, for what life has provided (whether it be spouse, monastery, the single state or something else) and be prepared to see it as response to a vocation. I say ultimately, because, to be sure, Christ showed no interest in being surrounded by yes-people. We have been graced with gifts, ambitions, and various types of discernment and will, and to refuse them is to refuse God's gift of life in its fullness. But they have to mesh in with life as it is, and in ninety-nine per cent of cases this means taking on board some things we would not have wanted. Similarly with the Christian way, we often waste too much time and energy in an endless attempt to achieve integrity of personal belief. Such a misdirecting of energy is of no use to anybody. It should always be there, but kept in proportion.

The Epistle to the Ephesians makes clear that each person's gift is fulfilled not through a personal intellectual quest alone, but through being integrated in the Body of Christ: 'We are no longer children, to be tossed by the waves and whirled about by every fresh gust of teaching ... [Christ] is the head, and on him the whole body depends. Bonded and knit together by every constituent joint, the whole frame grows through the due activity of each part, and builds itself up in love' (Ephesians 4).

I once sought advice from a countryman on how to build a stone wall. He was building at the time, amidst a pile of motley stones of all shapes and sizes. 'One golden rule', said he, 'is never to put a stone down once you have picked it up. It will fit well enough somewhere.' Trying to find just the stone for this or that funny hole could waste a whole afternoon. You simply press on. It is in this kind of sense that it can be proper for Christians to settle for what is given, whether it be doctrine, worship or church government.

There are two important qualifications to this, however. The first is that we have to strive to renew the Church and enable her to be better than she is. But there is a difference between ungenerous intellectual nit-picking, and positive criticism spoken in love and ready to accept not having its own way.

The second qualification is that this does not imply that *any* faith will do, that *any* practice is good enough, as if to say that the Church might believe in reincarnation, and had it done so, you would have had to settle for that, but as it happens to believe in the resurrection, that is what you will have to settle for. This is not what it means. It stems rather from the fact that although the current configuration of the Church may seem in many respects fortuitous, God has promised not to lead it completely up a gum tree, so however fortuitous and contingent some of Christian worship and faith may look, it is part of the deal to have a bias in favour of accepting that it was in some sense 'meant', and that God has had a big hand in its formation. This is a matter of fine tuning and proportion, not a blanket licence for credulity and abject submission. Simply a preparedness to go the extra mile or two. Believing that God has guided the Church in a special way ties in with the hope we found earlier on, when we favourably compared the present fragmentation of the Church with the worse fragmentation of Western society.

It is part of Alasdair MacIntyre's thesis that a society based on *emotivist* principles (that is, based on the capacity of each individual to choose his or her standpoints according to preference) is doomed to failure. The illusion of freedom-of-choice-for-all masks monopolies of unparalleled wanton power (such as international companies), and charismatic figures who enjoy esteem and respect which is largely undeserved (he cites the bureaucratic manager and the therapist as outstanding examples). In addition to this, the failure of emotivism to produce what it promises breeds in many a yearning for counterfeit certainties and systems that will provide answers on a plate.

The way forward out of this situation seems to depend on a fostering of small communities where the Tradition can be recovered and life can be lived once more with roots in a tradition-bearing community. While seeming to limit freedom, this in fact gives us the only freedom which is real. Nowhere else is freedom to be found. It seems an irresistible conclusion in Britain that the Church already provides such communities, the parishes of our land (and their equivalents).

Why communities? If all monasteries and convents disappeared for ever, the vast body of wisdom associated with them could not be preserved: it would disappear. It can only be understood by living it, and the only way to attempt to rediscover monastic spiritual insights would be for some people to start living the monastic life again. The same is true of piano-playing. It can be enjoyed from the outside, but can only be *lived* and carried forward on the inside of the piano-playing fraternity. Tradition is inseparable from the community which bears it. And because Tradition is, essentially, momentum, rolling forward by its own force and changing as it goes, it can only live in a community which has historical continuity. Our quest is therefore for community-in-momentum.

It is an ancient insight of the Church, and hence of Western civilization, that community is crucial in processes of education and formation. The collegiate life as lived for many centuries was not pursued merely out of practical convenience. It has always, until recently, been cultivated beyond the limits of practical necessity. Life in colleges (or, indeed, in peasant communities or different classes in society) has been collegiate to a degree, soaking individuals in the sharing of common humanity, and forcing them to come to terms with the fact that people are different. In the process we discover that many of our cherished attitudes are not so unnegotiable as we thought.

The decay of this can be seen in modern Anglican theological colleges, where a former common commitment to the daily office, for instance, has in some places been replaced by an approach in which each is supposed to find their personal path. The argument is that in the modern world people must find their own way. They will have to pray alone in the parish, so they had better get used to that now. They must work at finding suitable ways of prayer, and at developing self-discipline. While at face value this aim is both a realistic and a noble one, it contains fatal flaws.

First, I have tried to show elsewhere[29] that what we rather unromantically call the daily office is an essential given of the gospel. If this is so, and the whole of church history proclaims it is, then such theological colleges are in fact abandoning the gospel. In abandoning a collegiate understanding of worship, they are leaving the imaginative endeavours to individuals, when the gospel response would be a *corporate* exercise of imagination. But because we are out of touch with the staggering variety and imaginativeness which have characterized the daily office in its history, we don't consider that to be a possibility. We need to be purged of our stuffy and arthritic understanding of it which is quite out of tune with its true and ignored history. Because we are out of touch with the fact that the roots of daily prayer are corporate and indeed ecclesial, we settle too easily for a lesser substitute. If we believed in it enough, we would burn to establish corporate daily prayer in our parishes.

Secondly, we make a mistake in seeing theological training simply as a 'getting-in-gear' for the parish. That is only one of its functions. A further vital function of theological colleges is to steep the participants in gospel archetypes. Just as a music student at an English university will learn to write a chorale in the style of Bach, or even a Haydn symphony movement, so the student for the ministry has to be steeped in the collegiate archetype of the closeness of Christ with his disciples before the watershed of Pentecost, of the first Christians in Jerusalem, and of the early centuries of the Church. They will have the rest of their lives to wrestle with the parish situation, but if in that wrestling they can bring to bear only a feeble experience of the collegiate archetype, an essential element of the gospel is eroded.

Thirdly, this approach is leaving us with more and more clergy who cannot pray, and often suffering, furthermore, from a debilitating spiritual disorientation and superficiality. Something is clearly wrong in much current understanding of spiritual formation.

Fourthly, we have here a good example of the Church abandoning the Tradition not because this has had its time, but because the Church has failed to dig down to its roots and understand how the Tradition functions. Too lightly have we thrown something over because we have lost sight of its hinterland. No discipline of prayer worth its salt can be arrived at by individuals on their own—that is hopelessly idealistic. Such a thing can only be done in relation to a demanding community life.

What we have here in fact is MacIntyre's *emotivism* running riot: personal-preference religion, in which community pays the price for a form of self-indulgence which would not be tolerated in a marriage or an orchestra. As St Paul says to the Corinthians, What do you think you are doing? You eat for yourselves without waiting for the community. Why behave like this? You *are* the Body of Christ. Note that Paul does not say we have to create community. We are already that community, but behave as if we weren't. We are abandoning its archetypes.

I was once at a conference on the re-ordering of churches at which much was said about the building being a meeting-place for the people, in which the function of the sanctuary-area was to act as a focus. When eventually a clergyman protested that all the talk was of focuses and never of the symbolism of the altar, a lady got up and demanded that priests talk of things which ordinary people can understand. What he had said she could not understand. This raised a thunderous round of applause.

Where, you wonder, did the lady find the gospel of the understandable God? Jesus would have found it a great help. I thought of that disquieting passage in Job which ends: '. . . these are but the outskirts of his ways, but the thunder of his power who can understand?' (Job 26.14). Who can understand the mind of God? Asking for a religion which we can easily understand is unbiblical, but is typical of the spirit of our times. If allowed to have free rein, this would ultimately lead to a travesty, a trivialization, and pure self-indulgence, a feeding back to ourselves of our own desires. St Augustine says somewhere that it is in order to punish us that God gives us what we want. This is echoed in the Psalms: the Israelites in the wilderness complained about the arrangements. So God 'gave them their hearts' desire'—and it made them sick.[30]

The architects at this conference said that they could only respond to clients' requests, but could not take a lead in anything themselves (say in insisting on a ramp for the disabled). Clients on the other hand tend merely to ask for what they think they want. Hence the rarity of a well-designed altar. Often altars bear no clear relation to the available range of ground-symbols (such as table, altar, tomb) but are more like doodles with a flat top. In the transaction between congregations and architects (or church furnishers) something is often missing. It can't be explained in 'understandable' words. We can only be led through an experience of it, which can introduce it to us.

This can be easily proved. Ask someone to describe in an easily understandable way the person they love most, such that we can know them just as they are. It can't be done. An essential dimension will be missing. That dimension is just as important in re-ordering churches and in the symbolism employed. Such a dimension can only be found in a Church which realizes it is Tradition-bearing community.

Would such a community mean an end to pluralism and an ushering in of uniformity? As has already been noted, the Church has conserved more living Tradition than the world at large. Once again religious communities provide us with a good example, for they have lived with plurality for a long time. Benedictines, Franciscans, Trappists, Jesuits, Little Brothers and Sisters of Jesus—the list runs into thousands. The number of religious orders in the Roman Catholic Church is legion. Thousands of men and women have been inspired to found communities for the pursuit of this or that specialism. The differences between them are very deep. A Benedictine may well find it impossible to imagine how anyone could want to be a Franciscan, and no doubt the feeling can be mutual. Each can be so fired by the *charism* of his or her order as to be totally given to it.

And yet the paradox remains that each can at the same time be totally happy to embrace the plurality of the religious life. It is somehow a corporate plurality, founded on having been received by the Church. It is not an ant-heap of differing egos, it is ecclesial. It is a coalescing of plurality, where the differences of approach are between orders or companies within the whole, and not between individuals. It is a plurality which expresses different facets of one mystery, different ways of reaching a common goal, rather than a *pluralism* which takes different starting-points, using different means to attain different goals.

On the smaller scale, the pluralism of attitudes, beliefs and preferences is there for all to see in a religious community; yet there can be no strident beating of the personal drum. Of primary concern are the common life, the common good. And, as St Benedict intimates in his Rule, the holy art of listening takes precedence over the urge to speak. He envisages the community as a sacrament, where God is especially present in its deliberations, so that in listening to our brother or sister we are listening to Christ.

Traces of this tradition survive in the secular Church, but they are weaker. Plurality and freedom of thought are God-given gifts, but every gift requires a response. That response is expressed in speaking always with forbearance and charity, in preferring to believe the other right rather than oneself, and in always living and acting together with good will and commitment to the common life, and loyalty to commonly made decisions. Such is the price to pay for plurality, and it is a gracious one, a privilege to have it asked of us.

For people of the 1990s, however, this is an enormous price to pay, for it asks of us something which we don't seem to have to give, and that is something which has already arisen before, the attitude of reverence. Our world is an arena in which we shoot (and shout) our personal preferences at each other. All is fragments. Any standpoint is one among many. Nothing is sacred. And if nothing is sacred, nothing can be revered. Reverence therefore requires a leap of faith. At the other end of our leap stands the community of faith. This community can only be fully itself by means of the Tradition which carries it forward. Conversely, the Tradition can only be the Tradition in the community which passes it on.

The significance of the Tradition-bearing community (or, as I have called it, the community-in-momentum) is that only within this setting can we hope to be fully human. This community will follow no naive ideal but will be difficult and demanding, rich and rum, with unpredictable patterns of love and dislike, co-operation and disagreement, beauty and ugliness, achievement and failure; let none expect any other than a glorious and dirty struggle, with amusement and lamenting, inspiration and exasperation and, in short, not more of the *nice* side of human nature, but more of everything. That is what has to be meant by hoping to be fully human, at least in the short term.

Community-in-momentum is essential to our nature, and an essential arena for the very existence of thinking and reflecting. The fact that we can think and reflect shows that the Tradition-bearing community is there. Our problem is not its absence but its fragmentation.

Fergus Kerr in his book[31] harps on this as much as MacIntyre does. The inclination to isolate our inner working and to attribute to it a capacity to function prior to commerce with the exterior world is, as he puts it, 'the dream that tradition and community are dispensable'. There is 'nothing inside one's head that does not owe its existence to one's collaboration in a historical community. It is established practices, customary reactions and interactions, and so on, that constitute the element in which one's consciousness is created and sustained.'[32]

The need for Tradition-bearing community is demonstrated by MacIntyre far more thoroughly than is possible in this short chapter. Here I have simply presented some of his conclusions, while trying to show how they match up to experience.

If it is true that people always receive their world view from society, we Christians need a therapy to set us free from the mid-twentieth-century brainwashing which makes us believe in a pluralism of personal preferences exercised by supposedly private individuals, into a new state in which we realize that which we truly are, the Body of Christ. The result will be paradoxical: a Body of Christ not more restricted but (if we can take it) more human.

# CHAPTER 6 *Little Worlds*

Modern society is, in many senses, liberal. It prizes freedom, personal dignity, and openness to other points of view. It also prizes knowledge. Liberal indeed are the insights we derive from scholarly study and the ensuing capacity to test received practice in the light of empirical fact. Such knowledge is liberating in uncovering the lifegiving roots of reality. It also enables us to value and revere the infinite liberality of the world's diversity. So we shun easy answers, the lazy wish to have everything provided on a plate, and any desire to put faith in unreal little worlds of all too human manufacture.

What we have been saying about the Tradition seems to agree, and yet its position looks contradictory. It stands for order, and for apparent conformity. It even seems to want to prescribe how people should believe and how they should pray, putting ready-made 'packages' in their hands for the purpose.

By contrast, our variegated society will glory in the vastness of the cosmos, and the rich diversity of humanity. Look at the stars and the planets! Behold the breathtaking wonders of the universe! Its variety! Its versatility! Its surpassing of all human knowledge! Look at the cultural diversity of the modern world, and the seemingly endless creativity of humanity. Look at the kaleidoscope that makes up the Church. All is variety, every system is inevitably relative. To try to make the Church a circumscribed little world holding on to very specific doctrinal tenets is hopelessly blinkered. It is like standing before the wondrous majesty of the ocean, and rejecting the challenge of this bracing reality for a little water in a bucket. You cannot seriously propose to live in a little, circumscribed world, which is so clearly relative when seen against this stupendous backdrop!

All of this is undeniably true. And yet it is only one side of a paradox. Buckets are eminently useful things to have at the seaside. A boat, come to that, is nothing but a glorified bucket: without it the ocean would entrance us with its beauty while it quietly exhausted us and drowned us. But with a boat serious exploration of the whole ocean becomes a practical possibility.

In the same way, the Tradition draws itself in only in order to give its most concentrated attention to the mystery. It is like a spaceship. It may be small, indeed microscopic. It may succeed in surveying only a tiny fraction of the cosmos. But it will do a jolly lot more than any number of suicidal crowds of individual astronauts with no spaceship and poor co-ordination. This spaceship is a little world. Its inhabitants cannot go very far afield. But the only reason for its existence is that its eye is on the cosmos.

There is much uncomfortable truth in the frequent criticism of the Church that it has a tendency to become a *little* world, a *petit monde* of people who cannot perceive the narrowness of their own horizons. Too often Christians are a people who fail to allow their faith to be tested by the questions which the secular world constantly holds before them. This failure has many causes, amongst which must be counted fear, insecurity, lack of perception, provincialism, or sheer superficiality. Worship then becomes stuffy and hidebound, thinking stagnates, mission droops, and the message dies.

Failure to allow ourselves to be taken up in the greater life of the Kingdom, which is hidden like a seed in the everyday world, means we shrink down to a petty world held together by the mere keeping of rules. Then rise up the spectres of doctrinal sclerosis and 'correct' liturgy. When we are reduced to a constant preoccupation with the rules, the larger reality of the Tradition has been lost. There is no room then for true delight in each other and in the Lord who dances through the Gospels. There is only correctness.

In response, Christians are often proud of taking a critical and questioning stance vis-à-vis the Church. The Church for them is in constant danger of descending into churchiness, when it should in reality be self-effacing, refusing simply to live in its own little world. The Church, they feel, should be unconcerned about itself, should throw all self-concern to the winds; it should be challenged and challenging. In short, the Church is seen to consist merely of our human selves, far too corrupted by sin and selfishness. So, we feel, God's own attitude to it is ambivalent and critical, and ours should be too.

The problem with this stance is that if it fails to be accompanied by that reverence of which we have spoken, then it would need only a couple of generations for the Church's particular identity to have been seriously eroded, and the ultimate result would be no Church.

And yet we find it difficult to have the kind of love for the Church that is needed. How is it possible to love an institution with such a bad reputation? There is a very practical answer. We *need* to love it. Without love for the Church, we cannot hope to carry on for very long as Christians. In the psalms, Zion is traditionally used as a symbol of the Church, and of course one of the things which sustains both Jew and Christian is the love of Jerusalem as a symbol: 'her children love her very stones'.[33]

We are quite capable of loving the individuals who make up the Church, but have a built-in reserve against loving the Body itself, and for itself, as a privileged mode of the presence of Christ. But if we continue in this course, then our faith will become incredible, just as any family which behaved in that way would be an unconvincing example of family life; people who ignore their family life ignore it out of existence.

In practice this is usually recognized, and the result is a phenomenon which mirrors exactly the *emotivist* society in which we are set. Bits and pieces of the Tradition are taken up and put to use, according largely to preference, and affectionately held on to in tandem with the individual pursuit of personal stances. It is interesting to see how often people and institutions which pride themselves on their critical and adventurous stance fall back at certain points on traditional items, such as vestments, ceremonies, or the prizing of spiritual classics. But these are now fragments scattered like confetti in a fragmented community, whose ultimate source of authority is the autonomous individual, who is free to maintain a critical attitude towards the Church, a cautious embracing of an institution which is so prone to become absorbed in itself that any allegiance must be hedged about with conditions.

The inevitable result is that Christians are not held together: they have not a Church with a gospel to proclaim, but a Church with a stalemate, a mere arena in which different people pursue their preferences.

We are forced to return to a picture of the Church as a little world; not, however, as *petit monde*, but as *microcosm*. A circumscribed environment which replicates in its own way the realities of the cosmos; the spaceship whose micro-climate enables human beings to penetrate into reality to an extent that can be done in no other way. It is a diving-bell, which by means of carefully calculated limitations enables profundities to be measured which leave individual divers floundering miles above.

This little world merits the title microcosm because it reflects the cosmos. First, because it is open to the world, seeking to know it and learn from it, from the realities of 'ordinary' daily life, from the findings of the sciences, and from every aspect of the world in which it is rooted. Second, it reflects the cosmos by its contact with eternal realities, through contemplation of the divine mystery in prayer, liturgy and theology. This is brought about not least through effective symbol, the sacramental vocabulary of beliefs, practices and structures some of which were listed above in our brief digest of the content of the Tradition. This vocabulary is textured in an interrelated family of 'packages', structures of 'doing' which include ceremonies, rigmaroles, symbols, objects, time-cycles, doctrinal and theological formulations, symbolic persons, and so on. The Greek Orthodox 'package' is very different from those of the Church of South India, or of Roman Catholics in Venezuela. But they are all roads to the same end, which are not simply travelling in the same direction: they frequently meet.

Many details of the little world of the Church may seem fortuitous. It could have taken other forms. And yet it cannot be that *any* little world will do. The peculiar characteristic which distinguishes the Church from some other such little world as a spaceship or any kind of mutual support club is that it is a living entity, part of the timeless yet time-stamped vine which is Christ. It can only be our belief that he has given it to us.

We therefore seem bound to say that a very proper and necessary criticism of the Church has to be combined with a proper and necessary reverence, in which the Church is taken seriously as the Church, in all its particularity. Any failure to do so will lead to the end of the critics (through spiritual exhaustion) and the end of the Church (having been criticized to death).

Spiritual exhaustion is, not surprisingly, a problem of our age: laity often hang on by their fingernails, religious communities lose their sense of direction, clergy 'burn out'. That is what happens when you insist on living through a long and bitter winter with all the doors and windows open. Someone might reply that in central

67

Africa houses are only used to sleep in, and people live all day out of doors. But this proves the point: where the climate is friendly we can afford to expose ourselves; where it is hostile we have to take care not to overdo it.

Many people know the experience of finding it easier to be a Christian in the setting of a theological college, a prayer group, or a monastery than in a factory or a supermarket, or working in an office. Faith depends on community. There is a story of a young man who said he didn't need to belong to the Church in order to believe. His uncle said nothing, but took the tongs and removed the pieces of coal from the roaring fire and placed them one by one along the fender. They all went out. Faith needs community.

The ancient momentum of the Church speaks of the community of faith as a little world set apart, with its own style, norms and way of life. Although the oceans and the stars remain beyond our comprehension, and although the complexity and variety of modern society remain beyond our capacity to grasp them, yet this Momentum more than adequately compensates for that lack by embracing in itself both the natural and supernatural orders in microcosm.

Only through being limited can gunpowder produce a bang. Otherwise it gives a desultory, long-winded flicker. Only by creating the 'little world' of the house can we go out to tame and map the world. Otherwise the weather kills us off. Only by relating in the small unit of the family can we learn to be full participants in human society.

The Church is no different. Only by embracing the household of faith which in some sense keeps itself 'unspotted from the world' can we have the faith that will move mountains. That is the only way we can be that little, potent dash of yeast which leavens the whole lump.

When we postulate the necessity of a Tradition-bearing community, it therefore looks as though we need to accept limitations, but only for the very purpose of rising beyond all limitations, to find the perfect freedom of the gospel. Our society seeks a bogus freedom without limitations but fails to find it, and in the process dissipates too much of its energy. It is sometimes said that those who try to live without structure tend to waste a lot of time organizing their lives. Fergus Kerr puts it in terms of aspirations: 'If we never learn to own our finitude we remain tormented by a powerful inability ever to be satisfied by *anything*'.[34]

It seems to follow from all of this that the Church needs to take itself more seriously as Church, and to have sufficient confidence to treat its native peculiarities with the utmost seriousness. A parish should not be afraid of being a 'little world', so long as it is working hard at establishing how it and the daily world relate together.

The first question we should be asking is not: 'What challenges is the world putting before us?', or 'In what ways does God make himself known to us in secular life?'

Nor should it be the converse: 'What does the Church teach? What are the church rules?'

There is a question of a different order waiting for our attention, and it is this: 'What is born when the Divine presence in the Church and the Divine presence in the world are spliced?' A Church which cannot believe in itself as *microcosm* cannot get spliced; it is simply borne along in an ocean apparently benign, but ineluctably absorbing all things into itself.

Ruth Benedict, in her classic work *Patterns of Culture* first published in 1935, gives an illustration of what happens to people when their culture becomes fragmented:

> A chief of the Digger Indians, as the Californians call them, talked to me a great deal about the ways of his people in the old days ...
>
> 'In the beginning', he said, 'God gave to every people a cup, a cup of clay, and from this cup they drank their life.' I do not know whether the figure occurred in some traditional ritual of his people that I never found, or whether it was his own imagery. It is hard to imagine that he had heard it from the whites he had known ...; they were not given to discussing the ethos of different peoples. At any rate, in the mind of this humble Indian the figure of speech was clear and full of meaning. 'They all dipped in the water', he continued, 'but their cups were different. Our cup is broken now. It has passed away.'
>
> *Our cup is broken.* Those things that have given significance to the life of his people, the domestic rituals of eating, the obligations of the economic system, the succession of ceremonials in the villages, possession in the bear dance, their standards of right and wrong—these were gone, and with them the shape and meaning of their life. The old man was still vigorous and a leader in relationships with the whites. He did not mean that there was any question of the extinction of his people. But he had in mind the loss of something that had value equal to that of life itself, the whole fabric of his people's standards and beliefs. There were other cups of living left, and they held perhaps the same water, but the loss was irreparable. It was no matter of tinkering with an addition here, lopping off something there. The modelling had been fundamental, it was somehow all of a piece. It had been their own.[35]

We tend to have an ambivalent attitude towards ethnic groups who firmly defend their culture: on the one hand a rather naive respect and on the other what could be called a sense of pity for those caught in such a small world. We also have a tendency to regard such cultures as exactly commensurate, neat, tidy packages which ensure an ordered, and deadly inert, way of life. In reality the character of cultures varies enormously. Some are inert, ossified, some developing and innovating. Some succeed in ensuring what might seem to us a balanced mode of life, some do not succeed. Most have innate faults which lead to particular drawbacks. So some peoples are cheerful, some depressive, some make their way in the world, while some inhabit cultures which leave them vulnerable. This is part of the stock in trade of the anthropologist. What is common to them, however, is that such a culture forms the individual to such a profound extent that he or she in daily life simply lives out the culture.

That is one of the great foundation stones upon which any true individuality is built, and out of which innate gifts can reach their greatest fulfilment. The culture is a kind of music of which each individual plays their unique interpretation. It is, if you like, the 'Mighty Wurlitzer' on which each plays his or her unique music. A people without a culture, without a Tradition, has no instrument on which to play its music. It is just the same with our language, whose context and structure are almost entirely given, and yet each individual has his or her own way of speaking. We simply live out the language, yet we each put upon its standard forms our unique stamp.

If all that has been said in the preceding chapters is true, then there are some ways in which it can be said that the Church itself is a particular culture, a body of inherited particularities which decidedly inform its life, and express its identity. This 'culture' we could identify with what we have called 'the Tradition'.

It is necessary to be very exact in saying how the image of 'culture' can be used of the Church. Clearly we are not dealing with something which could replace, say, the culture of the Digger Indians. It is, rather, a precisely limited culture of which we are speaking, one of whose built-in properties is to key in with the cultures of human societies in such a way as to enhance them, not to replace them, and to be enhanced itself, but not replaced.

This subject is being much illuminated at present by the attention the mainstream Churches are giving to the question of the inculturation of liturgy. This is a process, given particular impetus by the Second Vatican Council, by which Christian worship may be enabled to become a true expression of a local culture, rather than some totally European and foreign importation. In southern Africa, for instance, this could lead to replacement of the typical Anglican robed choir by dancers in tribal dress, with native music accompanied by local instruments such as the marimba. It may even result in tribal robes replacing alb and chasuble. It would also lead to words and images which speak directly, where European ones would be foreign and incomprehensible (e.g. in countries where sheep are unknown, the words for other animals have to be used to speak of the 'Lamb' of God).

Some parts of the Church's inheritance are culturally determined in a relatively insignificant way. So, for instance, palm leaves used in Palestine on Palm Sunday become willow branches in northern Europe; kissing of icons would be difficult for Tanzanians, for kissing is not part of their culture. Church music and poetry is very notable for its local variety. Other parts of the Church's 'culture', although often geographically determined, cannot be easily adapted, however. Hence the problems with symbolism of broken bread in countries where bread has never existed, or languages where there is no suitable word for the Christian concept of love.

Our own history demonstrates that such a process of inculturation has always been vital and necessary. The famous letter of Pope Gregory the Great to St Augustine of Canterbury at the end of the sixth century assumes a process of inculturation which has typified the Western Church throughout most of its history:

> You, brother, know the usage of the Roman Church in which you were brought up: hold it very much in affection. But as far as I am concerned, if you have found something more pleasing to Almighty God, either in the Roman or in the Frankish or in any other Church, make a careful choice and institute in the Church of the English—which as yet is new to the faith—the best usages which you have gathered together from many Churches. For we should love things not because of the places where they are found, but places because of the good things they contain. Therefore choose from each particular Church what is godly, religious and sound, and gathering all together as it were into a dish, place it on the table of the English for their customary diet.[36]

We are faced with the same question today in our own Western industrialized societies, where much of traditional Christian symbolism and language ceases to mean anything for ordinary people.

If, however, this process is taken to its logical conclusion, we are left almost having to believe that the gospel and the Church consist of some abstract 'essence' which can float around like a spirit, looking for cultural bodies to inhabit. In a curiously paradoxical way, we would thus, by seeking to act on incarnational principles, be left with a profound compromising of the incarnation.

The truth, we must suspect, is more complex, slippery and

difficult to pin down. The gospel needs to come alive for people by coming to a new birth in ways that are native to their own culture. But the process runs in the other direction also: Christians and communities need to be 'inculturated' into the culture of the Church. For instance, they need to be able at least to some extent to enter into the culture of first-century Palestine if they are to engage in biblical exegesis. They need also to enter into the history of the Church, and the history of liturgy. If they fail to do that, and create worship which is purely of their own time, they are Christians without orientation, unable to gain a true self-understanding. Attempting to be a people without history is like trying to create a sculpture in two dimensions. History is outside us and takes us outside our culture to our own good.

We can see from all of this that inculturation in the liturgy is two-directional, and it is very difficult to work out how the two directions are to be held in balance. When has an Africanized liturgy not gone far enough, and when has it gone too far, so as to compromise fundamental symbols of the gospel? The principles here are as yet unclarified, and much work remains to be done, both by scholars and in the field, on this elusive and ambiguous question.

We have also to remember, in seeking to foster inculturation of the liturgy, that some cultures are inadequate, in fact all are to some degree, or they would not need the gospel. Some cultures lack adequate concepts of love, others adequate concepts of human nature, and so on. When we turn to modern Western society we find within it a plurality of 'cultures', if they can be so called, many of which are woefully inadequate in an unprecedented way. The modern urban way of life leaves many without any adequate experience of community, and without rituals and rhythms on which human nature depends. The Church's task here is, as much as anything, to help people create a culture, and this will partly be done by presenting them with things out of its storehouse. So, for instance, the act of gathering together in medium- or large-sized groups will be totally foreign to some people, and something they would probably need to learn. Again, candles are rarely if ever part of people's daily experience, yet are something that people respond to in worship without fail.

Although, therefore, it is vital that local communities be encouraged and enabled to evolve their own symbols, and their own

worlds of discourse and behaviour, this is not the whole story, and
if it were, the result, from the point of view of the Body of Christ,
would be a lame one.

When the Church engages with a culture, it should value and
expose itself to all that it can in that culture, and yet ultimately
remain conscious of the fact that *both* parties have to be prepared to
be changed in embracing each other. Inevitably the local culture
which adopts Christianity will have to change, for people are being
called to think and act in a new way, to undergo a conversion of
attitudes, and the new thing that results will not (or should not) be
a collection of transformed individuals, but a transformed culture
out of which they will live, think and speak: a new music in which
to express their virtuosity.

It is only in a very diagrammatic and illustrative sense that the
Church can be described as a 'culture'. Yet to describe the Church
in this way can be helpful in understanding its nature. If the
Church's culture has fragmented into a collection of only partly
intelligible dialects, we should expect Christians to show similar
symptoms to those manifested in the Digger Indian whose 'cup'
was broken: a sense of some irreparable loss, the disappearance of
something which constituted the very fabric of their life as a
people. This indeed sounds very like the situation of most Western
Christians today, and the more we compare the two situations, the
more we are affected by an eerie sense of the parallel being too close
for comfort.

Christians go out into the modern world like sheep to the
slaughter. The environment is so hostile to their beliefs, the world
so deafeningly proclaims that Christianity is one preference among
others of equal choosability, that it is supremely difficult to sustain
any convincing grasp on the faith. We are a people trying to live as
a new Israel but without any significant 'culture' to embody that
awesome citizenship. Like any who would foolishly think they
could start a monastery simply by following St Benedict's rule, we
are people trying to live according to principles, but principles
without much of a context. The image which often occurs to me as
I speak with people trying to pray and live by the gospel in such a
world, is that of trying to strike a match under water. We are trying
to be the people of God, but without the Church, naked and
exposed in our own little corners most of the time.

Once we begin to see the poverty of the Church's very own

culture, we feel that scales are falling from our eyes. We begin to see the baleful effects of this poverty on all sides. Everything is approached in such individual terms: *I* believe this, *I* do that; *my* faith is the foundation of *my* Christianity, and the acid test of parts of the faith is what they 'mean' to *me*. From ordinary layfolk to clergy, bishops and professors: everyone seems to do it. And as *my* achievements in these areas tend to be lacklustre, my individual relationship to the whole Christian enterprise inevitably feels rather wobbly.

Another thing connected with this is Wittgenstein's *bête noire*, those 'inner depths', those 'deeply personal' dimensions of ourselves which we claim as the ultimate source for our ability to believe, when in reality only the Body of Christ in all its particularity can give shape to our search for God. When people are deprived of that, it can be no wonder that they lose their faith, that even clergy feel assailed by darts of unreality, and sapped of spiritual vitality, and that the religious life seems to face so many unanswered and unanswerable questions. For the living context which should breathe life into our 'principles' is in bits and pieces, and reduced, for most people, to one hour on a Sunday morning. To be Christians in the modern world is to be a peculiar people, deviants indeed. How may such a peculiar people have any identity without a 'culture', how may they have any sense of purpose with so indeterminate a *patria*? Their sorry case makes it difficult even to live from day to day and sustain with perseverance the projects they undertake. One vivid illustration of this over-exposure to the chill winds of chance is the often troubled state of the clergy, and the current tragic situation regarding clergy marriage. Individuals should not receive all the blame when a vicar deserts his family to run off with a parishioner's wife: it is an inevitable fruit of a Church where many individuals have nothing to help them do any better than flounder along as individuals, totally exposed to the sharpest blasts the twentieth century can muster.

Closely related to this is a problem concerning the immanence of God. Today we rightly lay great store by the fact that God is to be found in his world and is not simply confined to the Church. Unfortunately we have created an imbalance here, by diminishing the role of the Church as a location of God's presence; we now regard the world as setting the main agendas. But how are we to recognize the 'God-ness' of the world without a standard to measure it by? How can we claim to recognize God in people without some 'neat' experience of him elsewhere? How shall we know what to look for? In order to be able to say to someone 'Your laugh is just like your mother's', we need to some minimal extent to have kept their mother's company. In practice we do have some idea of what we are looking for, because our picture of God has been greatly determined by our predecessors, who gave the Church, as Church, a greater importance in their life. But as future generations come one after the other, so all of this will gradually fade, until we shall be very unsure what we are trying to recognize in daily life. We are spending freely out of an irreplaceable deposit account. Eventually when all these received signposts have gone, we shall end with the opposite of our intentions: we shall turn daily life into God.

If we fail to give the Church's own life space to exist on its *own* terms, we shall lose the ability to see the divinity of the supermarket, the kitchen and the pub. Much of our talk about God being alive and at work in the world around us rings with much less conviction than it ought to. That is because it arises not out of a creative tension between two cultures, but an ill-thought-out capitulation to one of them. This capitulation is largely due to a very understandable reaction against the Establishment and stuffy churchiness. Greater care needs to be taken not to confuse churchiness and the Establishment with the Tradition. This is a case of 'overdone rebound'. These things and many more declare us to be a Church which has failed to engage with society from a position of cultural strength, but has simply taken on board, lock, stock and barrel, the *emotivism* of a personal-preference society.

The Body of Christ is a particular culture. It speaks its own language, has its own attitudes and modes of thought, and a received vocabulary of peculiar practices and paraphernalia. Once we are crystal clear about that, we can then begin to appreciate the capacity of these things for encounter and synthesis with the particular characteristics of any human society.

The incarnation is two-edged. God becomes man and in the process man becomes (is becoming) divine. False teeth provide a good image here. The Church has to have an upper set (the heavenly) and a lower set (the earthy); only so may its gospel hope to have any bite. It has to be familiar with its own culture as well as with that of the world. It has to take the transcendent seriously as well as the immanent.

The fact of capital importance is that the two 'cultures' should meet. If the 'world' has nothing to meet up against, there can be no dialogue. Where the Church's culture has been weakened and devalued belief becomes difficult, bits start to fall off, and ere long the whole lot slides down the precipice. The world is met by a Church with the incisiveness of a sponge.

If the Church is a particular culture, it will be obvious that entry into that culture can only be accomplished by stages. To outsiders some of it will feel foreign, even alien, and consequently it will be open to the risk of misinterpretation. We need, like Jesus, the courage to live with the frustration of being misinterpreted, and of accepting that some things cannot be said in a way that can be readily understood. The Church must have the courage to be itself, and to accept that those who embrace it will have to go through an apprenticeship in which they will gradually make it a part of themselves. If a married couple from Yorkshire bring up a young family in, say, Brazil, where the father has a job, they may be anxious that the children should grow up as English children. They may even be very keen that they should be proud natives of Yorkshire. There is no way those children are going to be formed into typical Yorkshire men and women if they stay in Brazil. They will have to go, say, to Leeds or Huddersfield. So it is with the Church. The Church is another country. Her children can only become her citizens by entering into her particular culture, so undergoing a process of conversion.

St Benedict puts this as one of the key concepts of his rule: *conversatio morum*, the conversion of manners and attitudes, something which is the process of a lifetime. The experience of a monastic novitiate gives some telling insights. If a community has been seriously depleted so that only one or two monks are left, it can be very hard work to conduct a novitiate for new recruits, and with some novices it would prove impossible; for this strange new culture, the monastic tradition, which the novice is seeking to understand, is so different that it can induce strong reactions. Anger, protest, knowing-better, all often emerge. Not only can the novice rebel against some things which on the surface seem nonsense (until he or she discovers their hinterland) but the challenge can also bring to the surface those inner conflicts and hurts which could continue to lie dormant in ordinary life. The larger the community, and the firmer its hold on its own tradition, the more the novice will be 'held', and the unleashed forces enabled to emerge in a controlled and positive way.

All of this, suitably translated, holds good for the Church at large. A Church which 'holds', and is not all over the place, will have one essential ingredient for that manifold process by which, throughout our lives, we are converted into that which we were meant to be. Such a Church will be a listening Church, but sufficiently confident in its tradition not to collapse before every lobby that comes along. Needless to say, we are not talking here of looking for any old straitjacket, but for that living, supple manifestation of the divine love which is the Momentum of the Church. It is no straitjacket, for, like Benedict's monasticism, it is changed in the process of changing others. The very newest monks are among those whom the abbot has to consult, and he has to treat their views with as much seriousness as anybody's, in all the running of the monastery.

In the modern world at least, the Church of Christ is another country, which moreover has its own right kind of patriotism, as the traditional liturgical texts for the feast of the Dedication tell forth in such vivid images. 'Those who trust in the Lord are like Mount Zion, which cannot be moved, but stands fast for ever. The hills stand about Jerusalem: so does the Lord stand round about his people, from this time forth for evermore' (Ps. 125). Such images are weak in the consciousness of Anglicans, to the benefit of no one. The power of Christian patriotism is unique: the Body of Christ is like no other country on earth in that while having such a strong sense of its own peculiar citizenship it values so highly those who are not its official citizens, all God's children on this earth, that its relations with those outside itself can only take the form of love, and an eagerness to serve, to listen, and to learn.

Finally, it is just for them as much as for anybody that it takes supremely seriously its worship and prayer, liturgical and non-liturgical, that it offers it up day by day, a cultural inheritance pursued with assiduity, love, and joyful commitment, strewing across the cosmos a song that will summon all God's children to him by its sheer strength. This song is the song of a Church which is glad to be itself because it has accepted itself.

# CHAPTER 8 *The Practice*

When a mother tends a baby, she is there as a practical necessity. Without someone to tend him, the baby would not survive. The arrangement, however, is more than a practical one. Mother, if all is well with her, takes pleasure in tending the baby. The baby also, often (although not always) takes pleasure in being attended to. It can therefore be said of this relationship that good is achieved at two levels. It is achieved *externally*, in that nappies get changed, food is provided, shelter, warmth and safety are assured for the infant. But good is also achieved *internally*, in that the simple business of relating is a good thing in its own right. The internal good is the joy mother and baby have in each other. So in this kind of activity we can say that its pursuit brings external fruits and internal fruits.

Another example could be the restaurateur who is solely interested in how much money he can make from his customers. His slavery to external goods is to be contrasted with the attitude of the restaurant-owner who, while glad to pay his way, also takes pleasure in seeing all his guests enjoy their meals, going out of his way to please purely because it gives him pleasure and joy to make of his meals a work of art in which all can take pleasure.

Some activities only produce external fruits. Among these would be cleaning your teeth, filling in a tax form, or buying up a business. In none of those is the central object (teeth, tax or business) a good to be pursued purely because the pursuing of it is good. There are ulterior, functional motives for pursuing it.

Alasdair MacIntyre, in drawing attention to this question, coins the term 'practice'.[37] A practice is an activity which is pursued for the purpose of both external and internal good. The external good is a practical, functional end. The internal good is an intimate part of the thing itself. Externally, the baby is kept clean and happy; internally there is another (and greater) good which goes no further

79

than these two people. So the mother will say that loving her child is good because it is very, very good.

But there is more to a 'practice' than this. The participants are driven by a desire to excel. This leads to a gradual extending and enlarging of the 'practice'. Hence the history of European painting, or the forward-pressing movement of any living tradition.

Closely related to this is the fact that a 'practice' tends to have inherited standards of excellence, and rules to which the newcomer has to submit. That is quite clear in football (it is not easy to change the rules), architecture (you have to learn how to make a building stand up and stay up *and* be good to look at), or farming (cows can't wait for you to learn how to milk). A 'practice' therefore involves being prepared to accept the authority of the standards which at present obtain; in other words it requires an apprenticeship in which we must expect to be changed. MacIntyre takes a musical example: 'If, on starting to listen to music, I do not accept my own incapacity to judge correctly, I will never learn to hear, let alone to appreciate, Bartok's last quartets.'[38]

It is part of MacIntyre's thesis that the notion of a 'practice' is on the decline in the modern world. This can be readily recognized in many fields. It is more likely nowadays, most people would say, for something you buy in the shops to have been made for a quick profit than for pride in turning out well-made goods. In education, the study of English grammar has greatly declined. Along with that has gone a finely tuned tradition of acceptable English usage, of a kind in tune with our literary tradition. Formerly, many *bêtes noires* were easily recognizable, and shibboleths abounded. Now that has been replaced by a chaos of non-grammarians. The baleful result is not merely the loss of an aesthetic approach to language, nor is it merely the fact that colleges have to cope with students who cannot write English or cope with the structures of a foreign language. The most ominous result is that thinking itself is impaired. The language is losing precision, and with it the ability to think with anything other than broader brush-strokes. As Wittgenstein so rightly points out, language is not an encoding or incarnating of thoughts which have already happened: whether mental or spoken, language *is* our thinking.

Communities can lose the ability to sustain 'practices' for a variety of reasons. The causes are usually creeping ones. Hence the loss of monasticism at the Reformation, the disappearance of sacrosanct concepts of justice in Hitler's Germany, and the collapse of tribal and local cultures the world over in modern times.

If such has happened in the 'world' today in many domains, then we hardly dare look at the Church, to see what devastation has occurred there.

To see the Church's internal life as 'good because it is very, very good' is now to an alarming extent a marginal attitude. Here we are not talking about mere churchiness. If a mother takes pleasure in tending her baby, that internal good may be deficient if it derives merely from a pleasure in tending babies. In that case any old baby will do, any old nappies. The crucial matter is that it is *this* baby which is important, before any other. Then the attention is not on the tending. It passes beyond it to a meeting which is of absolute value.

In church life there can be a mere churchiness, or a mere delight in churchy things, churchy talk, and cultic escapism. But the internal good of which we are speaking is of a different order altogether. It is something so fundamental to the whole Christian enterprise as to affect its prospects in all regards. When the traditions of a language are not prized for themselves the process of thinking can become debilitated. When music is not loved for itself, the performer will fail to touch the audience. When a baby is not loved for itself, the care it receives will lose a whole essential dimension. When a Church ceases to value God and pursue him for his very self all its other activities become impoverished and unconvincing. No wonder the Church of England fails to produce vocations for the religious life. Its attention is held by external goods, while monasticism's whole *attrait* is for the internal.

Being a Christian must be reckoned amongst the highest callings that human beings can receive. As such it must merit at least to qualify as a 'practice', and certainly not less than that. This being so, we shall expect that Christians will pursue both the internal and external good in the Church's life. So, for instance, they will prize the Church's worship as being good because it is very, very good, they will delight in it because they delight in God, and believe he delights in them. Naturally it will therefore be performed with such care and reverence as are accorded to things of supreme importance. No effort will be spared in ensuring its excellence, according to the nature and means of the community. And that will be good not because the people are lovers of liturgy, nor because

81

they particularly wish to convert people through it, nor for any other reason. It will be good because it is very, very good, a delight, a joy, meet and right so to do. Inseparable from the liturgy is the pilgrimage of prayer, the contemplative pursuit of God and the abiding consciousness of his presence. He, after all, is the one who is in charge. Our road leads to Christ and thence to unity with the Father.

The topsy-turvy methods of the gospel mean that this very internal good, if such it truly is, will invade and infect all external goods that are sought. Even administration will be transformed.

If we aspire to pursue excellence, whether it be in worship, in the way we look after our church building, or in the practice of Christian 'card games', this excellence is not at all incompatible with informality. When I was a parish priest we built up a large choir of girls and boys through having a weekly club in church before choir practice. We had snooker in the Lady chapel, darts in the vestry, a football machine by the font, and badminton in the nave. But the children knew that the sanctuary did not come into the bargain, and was to be treated with reverence. And often there was teaching, and always prayer. The services on Sunday were offered by all with a carefully-evolved balance between informality and reverence, and it was precisely because great care was taken over the things of God that taking liberties with his house was imaginable. It was part and parcel with the life-giving bonds of the community's eucharistic life. This is very different from some dual-purpose churches where parties and celebrations are held before the altar for people who have not yet learnt what the altar stands for. Then the Church merely proclaims to the world that it stands for nothing different, nothing new. Juxtaposition of altar and daily life only has power if the altar already is a powerful and familiar symbol. For the very sake of those who are outside the life of the Church, familiarity has to be kept within the family.

More powerful than such sanctuary-parties will be a church which is well kept and has its potential users in mind, according to whatever is locally appropriate, where care is taken over furnishings, symbols, and what is made available, and which looks lived-in and welcoming. These things take such very little effort that when a church is looking down-at-heel, fusty and dull, the building can only give the game away that the people of this place do not care for the 'culture' of the Church in the way that a mother does with her baby, or anyone does with the things which belong to a person they have a passion for. Of course, the onlooker may not even get in. Unlocked doors, a paid guardian and a touch of heat in winter are possible in many places where people are at present locked out.

People instinctively expect, even if they cannot put it in words, that Christian worship and its attendant paraphernalia will be treated as a 'practice'.

The Church embraces not one, however, but a whole range of 'practices'. *Service* of our neighbour and of our society is seen today very much as a 'practice', and rightly so. *Community* too has to be understood as a good worth pursuing for its very own self: this is known as the building up of the Body of Christ. *Study*, reflection and honest enquiry are also essential to that Body's health, and are to be held as prized and sacrosanct in their own right: this corresponds to being wise as serpents. Meekness such as that of the doves will not do on its own.

It is not enough, however, that such things be highly prized. Pursuit of an internal good carries with it a feeling that any infringement of it would be taboo. It is not simply good for the concert pianist to play to the best of her ability: to her it is unthinkable that she could ever do otherwise. For the mother, loving care of her child is more than simply something worth taking seriously: a mean description such as that would make her shudder with shame. A judge, put under political pressure to adjudicate in favour of certain parties, would (we hope) reply: 'over my dead body'.

When we speak, therefore, of a 'practice', we are understanding such a degree of unity between the pursuer and that which is pursued, as to be the highest and most complete kind of unity that can be possible. The allowing of any chink in that unity is unthinkable. That chinks do occur in the 'practices' of the Church is a fact of history. Different ages fail in different ways, obviously. The later Middle Ages were hot on liturgy, not always so hot on honest inquiry or social justice. Today we have a tendency to understand mission and service as 'practices', but worship and prayer as mere producers of external goods; and as for community, for all our talk about it we fail to treat it as a 'practice', but more constantly reflect the individualism and fragmentation of our society.

Here we discover the extent to which we are crippled, for

MacIntyre is insistent in pointing out that a 'practice' is only possible within a tradition, and tradition is only possible within a community which lives within a continuity. When those things become weakened, one thing that tends to fill the gap is sentimentality. The eighteenth-century deist view of God was deeply sentimental. Victorian religion was even more sentimental in its own way. We ourselves may well go down in history as an age of spiritual immaturity and sentimentality. Much modern argument and apologetic for particular positions can be surprisingly sentimental. This can only be the case where, in the absence of a common tradition, there are no shared bases for discussion on so many topics, and therefore debate comes to be dominated by feelings. Feelings too have to fill that gap in Christian art which is left by the lost challenge of the Tradition. Much modern worship would be better left undescribed. Many parish priests, grown men, can be unbelievably sentimental in their sermons and their prayers. It is all a *substitute*, compensating for the lack of a vigorous culture.

It is perhaps in the area of a *community* that many of our worst ills in this regard are to be found. An example would be a certain kind of individualism which prevails amongst the clergy. The meetings of a deanery chapter can so often display not only a wide disparity of views, which is no bad thing in itself, but also a failure to get beyond that, so that each member keeps his or her opinion, and carries on with his or her projects just as they personally prefer. In such circumstances it is not surprising to find a lack of responsibility with regard to projects undertaken by a deanery as a body. The whole of the Church of England is riddled with such irresponsibility, a childlike inability to co-ordinate. There is no true community because there is little sense of 'practice'. So parish team ministries have gained a reputation for being unable to work well. Their aim is to establish 'collaborative ministry' for a pastoral area. Although we have used the term 'collaboration' above, it has to be said that mere collaboration cannot be enough. Any religious community could testify eloquently to that! Parish clergy are not called to be monks and nuns, but the parallels between the two are closer than might be thought, not least because of the profound human frailty that undermines any co-operative endeavour. Life in a religious community makes you very much a realist on that one. *Collaboration* for clergy is a non-starter in most cases. Something more radical is needed, something which we once had and have lost, and that is the model of the clergy as a corporate body under the bishop. If a team ministry is to work, its participants will have to see commitment to the corporate endeavour as something of so high a value that any infringement of it would be unthinkable. Many things may have to be sacrificed for the achievement of such a corporate unity. Here is an example.

The religious community to which I belong has smaller houses in various places. The members of a house will not make grand changes as they think fit. Even small changes, say to the timetable or to customs, will hardly be undertaken lightly, or without consultation in the wider community. This is not due to crude reasons of obedience as such, nor to pusillanimity or the discouraging of initiative and creativity, but rather because the sense of belonging to this community is so strong that things which might seem straightforward in the secular world are not so straightforward here. At its best, we see in this example a giving up of personal preferences because they simply pale in significance compared with the benefits reaped by living as community. Religious communities often fail at this, of course, and few would wish to hold themselves up as shining examples for the rest of the Church. But experience of the sacramental nature of that community which can result does throw a very revealing light on the way the Church at large endeavours to order its life. Mere collaboration is a hopelessly inadequate ideal, presupposing a pooling of personal preferences, or a helpful overlapping of separate spheres. Such idealistic tools assume the absence of sin, or its presence in only moderate quantities. They are useless with typical clergy! It is of the nature of the clergy to be a corporate body, as can be seen from the New Testament onwards until very recent times.[39]

Say that at a deanery chapter and you will get a quick reply: 'It's totally unrealistic!' The fact, however, that we see it as almost impossible to contemplate is ultimately a sign of the inadequacies of our formation. Our aspirations are stunted. True, the current level of plurality in the Church makes it all exceedingly difficult. But that is an insufficient reply on its own. Again we are being content to erode a fundamental principle of the gospel.

Until relatively recently the ministerial life was naturally collegiate—it was assumed to be team-work. In the modern parish the immediate consequence of this has to be team-work for the laity, clergy and other parish ministers together. That is where the reality of the collegiate Church will be lived out day by day, and it is right that it should be a top priority for our times.

Behind that, however, stands a majestic gospel archetype: the college of the apostles. Clergy may not be able to meet together very often. But they could transform the quality of the occasions when they do. They could show greater forbearance and willingness to listen, greater ability to co-operate, greater eagerness to overcome their often very wide differences. And the ministers of the Church could do much more to love and care for each other, and to be one in spirit in situations where it is often very difficult to gather as a corporate body.

If clergy learn, as hopefully they do, that their unity and co-operation with all members of the parish community in a team effort make demands on their forbearance and their attention to others, then the same virtues need to be applied to their relationships with the other clergy, whatever the obstacles in the way.

It would be difficult to imagine a Last Supper at which the Lord prayed: 'Father, may they collaborate even as you and I collaborate.' And no amount of management consultants can fill the hole left by a lost chunk of the gospel.

The price of restoring that chunk is high. Collegiality as an ideal whose infringement would be taboo can only be bought at the cost of giving second place to many of our cherished individual preferences, opinions and plans. What is gained, however, is of such surpassing value as to be more than worth the sacrifice and pain we may at times feel.

The life of the Church is good because it is very, very good, the worship of the Church is so essential as to be prized with every fibre of our being, and the pursuit of the good of the Church purely for itself, by being the road to unity with the Father, is good to a degree which exceeds the capacity of language to express it.

# CHAPTER 9 *Abba*

A serious question lurks menacingly in the background now. If the Church is a distinctive world with, in some senses, a culture of its own, this would be difficult to envisage in a Church run on democratic lines. How, then, would decisions be made?

This question has been faced and answered in the New Testament, and in the subsequently evolving Tradition it turned out that decision-making in the Church is only truly Christian when it takes the form of a 'practice'. That is, if decision-making is seen purely as a means to producing ends which are external to it, then it will corrupt. It has to be something which is a good in its own right, sacramental, as it were, of the essence of the Church.

This can be seen in the growing unease at the functioning of the Church of England's General Synod. It is coming to be said in many quarters now that the Church is no mere democracy. What do we mean by this? It might suggest perhaps a need to concentrate the 'power' in fewer hands.

A great deal of light can be thrown on this by the monastic tradition, in its understanding of how the life of a religious community is ordered. This had evolved to a degree of considerable subtlety by the time of St Benedict, and was subsequently developed further. Whether we speak of Franciscans, Jesuits or most of the other main orders, the essential principles remain the same. The picture that emerges is of particular fascination in the light of modern struggles.

We will stay for our example with the tradition out of which the Rule of St Benedict was born. Here the abbot represents Christ in two ways. First of all, he represents Christ to the community. He is a person set apart, like any of the Church's ministers, to hold before the community the Word which comes from God. This role is understood as quasi-sacramental.

But the abbot is also the opposite, representing the community to God. Here he represents Christ by imitating his obedience. It is because the superior is obedient himself that the community will listen to him. Otherwise conflict would ensue. Through his own obedience he gains the community's ear, and is thus able to be seen as one with them, leading them in obedience to the Father. 'Let him who would be first among you be the servant of all.' Indeed, the model is the suffering servant of Isaiah.

Most parish priests will know what this means. No one can see the strains and suffering, and even the torment that a parish priest has sometimes to bear. So many responsibilities, so many clamouring voices, and so great a feeling of inadequacy, and guilt at many things unsatisfactorily done or still waiting for attention. It is particularly when many things all happen at once that the experience can be sharpest. In the same morning a vicar can be struggling at the typewriter to meet a deadline, then overwhelmed by someone's sudden tragedy, then receive a phone call complaining over some small matter like a flower-arrangement, and all the while be weighed down by a looming meeting at which he will have to cope with anger over the state of the church boiler. No one who has not been in such a position of responsibility can understand the almost impossible emotional stress it can impose. Others cannot see the multitude of lines all converging on the person who stands at their eye.

It is the same for the superior of any religious community, concerning not simply relations within the community, but also all the relationships and responsibilities regarding people outside, people who may be numbered in thousands. Anyone in a position of pastoral leadership has to be prepared for the model of the suffering servant, to receive with as much grace as is in them all the dark stuff which flies in their direction, and to receive it and respond to it in a spirit of generosity and obedience.

When it comes to the making of decisions, the abba is anything but an autocrat. He or she listens to all that the community has to say. St Benedict insists that the abbot has particularly to listen to the youngest, because the Holy Spirit is sovereign and speaks in the young as well as the old. All of this speaking and listening has to go on in an extended 'parley' until something comes to birth. It is then that the abbot gives it voice, as expressing the common will of the whole community. Not all will agree, but all will be committed to it, because the unity of the community is, in most cases, such a highly-placed ideal, that it is of greater value than little victories on this or that. The decision, indeed, is a mere external good. The internal good, on the other hand, is of infinite worth. It is the discussion itself. It may have had heated moments, or moments of conflict. But as a whole it is a sacrament of the life of the community, extending it and deepening it as it goes.

This is nothing peculiar to monasteries. One of the extraordinary things about the ARCIC statements on Ministry and Authority in the Church is the closeness of the parallel between them and not only the New Testament but also the Rule of St Benedict. Uniting all three is a common vision of *episcopé* (oversight) in which the spiritual father represents Christ to the community. He represents by the will of the community, over against the community, Christ's claims on the community's and each member's life.[40]

There are church council meetings or other groups where this can and does take place. In addition, a parish priest can often have the sensation when he is preaching that he is not simply giving his own thoughts, but bringing to maturation things which have been gestating in the congregation. There is something of this in a Quaker meeting where a vote is never taken, but reflection goes on until all are of a common mind. The difference there would be that the abbot, priest or bishop plays a role which is more than that of mere chairman. It is a sacramental role which carries with it a special kind of authority which can enable the whole enterprise to be elevated to a plane where it becomes uniquely Christian, uniquely ecclesial. The danger in presenting such an ideal portrait is that it might look too good to be true, and indeed that is how it often works out: it is as open as anything else to trouble, through the cussedness and frailty of even the most pious Christians (perhaps particularly those).

So far we have used masculine imagery because it has made for brevity, but if it were not redressed, this would be a distortion. The patristic writers often speak of this role as being like that of a mother as well as a father. The sixth-century Rule of the Master says that the abbot has to have the tenderness of a father and the love of a mother. The quasi-sacramental nature of his role is bound up very much with this image of fatherhood and motherhood. The words 'abbot' and 'abbess' both derive from 'abba', the word which Jesus used to address the Father. This role has been exercised by both men and women in their respective ways (the women have perhaps always outnumbered the men). The Tradition often describes it in terms of spiritual fatherhood, and for the sake of brevity I shall use that term in what follows, taking it to include spiritual motherhood as well.

One of the primary functions of the bishop is to teach. He carries the pastoral staff of the shepherd, and he is called 'Father in God'. Like the superior of a religious house, he needs the qualities of a father and of a mother. This is the key to the nature of his teaching. It is not so much that of the schoolteacher as that of the mother and father.

The life of the home is based not on instruction nor on autocracy, but simply on family life. Through it the child is enabled to enter fully into the life of society. This is not achieved through instruction, but through that mutual commerce of father, mother and child, part of whose genius is listening and being listened to. In the spiritual fatherhood of any Christian community, the community's life courses through the father's veins until a moment comes when this meets with all that is in him to produce a new 'Word', which he utters with the authority of Christ. Not that mistakes won't be made, or wrong decisions taken, but the product of greatest worth is not the decision, but the process. 'May they be one even as you and I are one.'

Monasticism has tended to articulate this more clearly than the secular Church, perhaps because its attention has been directed so much more to this kind of issue, given the nature of its life. But this sacramental understanding of the life of the Christian community has always been tacitly understood in the Tradition of the Church. It is there for all to see in the letters of Paul and the example of Christ. Like any good teacher, Jesus was more interested in helping people discover things for themselves than in handing out instruction. He also knew what was possible with certain people and what was not. He knew there was a time to speak and a time to keep silence. Yet he could never be described as non-directive. The gospel was not decided by a show of hands. In the patristic age this was carried forward. St Jerome offered the following advice on being a bishop:

> Be obedient to your bishop and welcome him as the parent of your soul. . . .
> This also I say, that the bishops should know themselves to be priests not lords. Let them render to the clergy the honour which is their due that the clergy may offer to them the respect which belongs to bishops.

There is a witty saying of the orator Domitius which is here to the point: 'Why am I to recognize you as leader of the Senate when you will not recognize my rights as a private member?' We should realize that a bishop and his priests are like Aaron and his sons. As there is but one Lord and one Temple, so also there should be but one ministry. Let us ever bear in mind the charge which the apostle Peter gives to priests: 'Tend the flock of God that is in your charge, exercising the oversight not by constraint but willingly as God would have you; ... not as domineering over those in your charge but being examples to the flock.'[41]

The Church of England perhaps needs to take more seriously the role of spiritual fatherhood/motherhood. The model for General Synod should not be the Houses of Parliament, but the sacramental mystery of the Body of Christ, in which all decision-making is seen as more than mere debate. There will still be passions and conflict, the cut and thrust of debate, and battles to be fought. But when the discussion itself is seen as sacramental, when each is ready to hear Christ speaking in the other, then it will be transformed. The dialogue will also have a special character where it is carried on with the Church's chief shepherds, the bishops. The Church is not led by civil servants, but by fathers-in-God. These are no mere executive officers of a parliament, but convergence-points of the Church's Christlike nature. A Church which has no understanding of spiritual fatherhood is a eunuch-church. The same is true of any local Christian community.

Placing greatest value in the debate itself brings with it a corollary. All decisions taken are decisions of the whole community. Some may disagree strongly with decisions taken, but they embrace them without demur in normal circumstances because the common will and the common good are of infinitely greater worth than particular opinions on this and that. We may still wait for our moment to open up the subject again, and be quite open about our different opinion (and certainly not covert about it), but in all our actions we abide by what has been agreed without murmuring, partly because of the high value we place on the unity of all, and partly because it is a salutary reminder of the depths to which we can delude ourselves in assessing our own rightness. Gilbert Shaw, one-time warden of the community of the Sisters of the Love of God at Fairacres, uttered on his deathbed some words of advice which are wise words for any Christians to listen to; these words also show clearly that what we are talking about is nothing soft or uncritical, but robust and without illusions:

The Holy Spirit will never give you stuff on a plate—you've got to work for it.

Your work is LISTENING—taking the situation you're in and holding it in courage, not being beaten down by it.

Your work is STANDING—holding things without being deflected by your own desires or the desires of other people round you. Then things work out just through patience. How things alter we don't know, but the situation alters.

There must be dialogue in patience and charity—then something seems to turn up that wasn't there before.

We must take people as they are and where they are—not going too far ahead or too fast for them, but listening to their needs and supporting them in their following . . .

Seek for points of unity and stand on those rather than on princples.

Have the patience that refuses to be pushed out; the patience that refuses to be disillusioned.

There must be dialogue or there will be no development.[42]

This tradition shows that those who are called to spiritual fatherhood and motherhood in the Church are not concerned with either power or control: they are graced bearers of the Word within that lifestream which is the community's search for the will of God.

It may well be asked, if this is so, how it is that monasticism can place such importance on obedience. The word 'obey' comes from the Latin *ob-audire* which literally means to listen. The etymological origin of obedience is connected with listening. In Greek *hup-akouo* is just the same. Romanian is a language very close to Latin, and for 'obedience' it has the word *ascultare*, which is the very word with which St Benedict begins his rule: 'Listen, my son'. Obedience is central to the monastic tradition, and its primary sense is that of listening. It is very interesting that in modern times we should have come to the realization that listening is at the heart of good counselling. To be a good counsellor is to be one who listens. So it is with the nun or monk. In this way the monastic tradition can speak of *mutual* obedience among the brethren. Chapter 72 of the Rule of St Benedict reminds them 'to give one another precedence [Rom. 12.10]. Let them bear with the greatest patience one another's infirmities, whether of body or character. Let them vie in paying obedience one to another.'[43]

We listen partly in order to learn. In having a listening attitude to my brother or sister I am wishing to put myself in their shoes, to attend to and value what they have to say, in the expectation that it may change me. When this reaches the point of being asked to do something, it means I am willing to respond and do it, because any inconvenience it may cause, or any positive practical results it may have, are only of relative importance. The buried treasure of great price is the actual commerce of request and response, and its sacramental effect on the relationships between individuals and in community.

Many religious communities will have in their number one or perhaps more who are noted for their ready, unmurmuring response to any request, and their willingness to help wherever help is required. Such demands are so constant in a monastery or convent that it is a sign of great grace when a person can be so generous and devoid of grumbling. Many others who aspire after such a virtue know how difficult it is to pursue, and how far they are from attaining it. Generosity of response, and giving more than is asked of you, are things that few achieve wholeheartedly. But the aspiration after those things, however much we fail, is a vital contributor to the building up of community.

On the other hand, most communities will know how the habit of refusing requests, or carrying them out with bad grace, is undermining and discouraging to all. Every time we say No without good reason we pull a brick out of the foundations of community. In the process we also reject the possibility of hearing Christ's voice and summons in the other person, and so do harm to ourselves. Habitual disagreement or 'no's' introduce large cracks which can sap a community's vitality.

No one dare speak about a matter such as this with a clear conscience: the speaker himself will always come under judgement from his own words; and yet in discussing the mystery of Christian obedience these things have to be named.

The sacramental effect of request and response finds a perfect model in the annunciation of the angel to Mary, where we see that interchange of gentle request and generous response which are so central to the gospel.

Obedience as it is popularly understood, however, merely means doing what you are told, toeing the line, diminishing yourself for the purposes of earning money, of getting some job done, or simply out of fear. We think perhaps of the member of the Foreign Legion made to carry a knapsack full of bricks through a sweltering Sahara, or, perhaps closer to our experience, of the parents driven to the point of having to lay down the law to erring children. We associate obedience with jumping into dutiful action at the snap of somebody else's finger. Such ideas are light-years away from the proper meaning of Christian obedience, which is part of the search for that greatest of all freedoms, the freedom that only Christ can give. It is concerned not with limitation but with opening up, with learning to be open to the other, open to our neighbour, open to Christ. This can only have meaning in the climate of love, the climate of the gospel. 'If you love me you will do what I ask.' Our eyes are not on our own freedom. They are on the other.

This obedience asks of us a readiness to learn, as well as a readiness to unlearn, in Benedict's process of *conversatio morum*, a conversion of your way of living. In this joint search others will also be obedient to you, as each helps the other to discover his or her true self. The fruits are not at the functional level of the work that is enabled to get done, but in the very response itself.

If a superior says to a nun or monk: 'What would you say if I asked you to go and found a house in Peru?', the person's heart might sink with utter dismay. Yet he or she will know several things: first, that the dismay has to be tested by going through the challenge, not avoiding it; second, that the bias is towards finding good reasons for *not* being sent, rather than for reasons why they *should* be sent.

There is, of course, the ultimate appeal to conscience, which has to be respected. But appeals to conscience need to be treated with extreme wariness. They are not something to be trigger-happy about, as can be so readily revealed in a religious community, where members can have a relentless knowledge of each other, enough to reveal how mixed are all motivations. To invoke conscience is to exercise an awesome responsibility. Conscience and 'principles' are wonderful things: their big drawback however is that they are found only amongst sinners. Christian obedience seeks to overcome that sinful warp by a passionate bias in favour of 'listening'.

A third consideration which will be present in the mind of the brother or sister is a willingness to believe the superior stands in the place of Christ and speaks with his voice. There will therefore be an expectancy to counteract the dismay: an expectancy that grace will be given, so that they will be enabled to fulfil what is being asked. And through it they will be enlarged.

Many people might respond that this is a marvellous ideal, but depends too much on the 'abba' being a good one. What happens when he or she is a bad one? Several responses can be made to this: *(1)* While in particular instances in history this office has been corrupted, the overall effect *on balance* has been more favourable to preserving *episcopé* as seen in the New Testament and the early Church, than the various attempts to represent *episcopé* according to a strictly democratic model. In the long-term view, it has achieved the desired ends more completely than straight democracy would have done. *(2)* The life of a community should not be allowed to get to the stage of rebellion against a leader in the first place. All are responsible for it. *(3)* A modern spiritual father knows that his flock are free—his authority rests on consent and trust, and misuse of that will damage the workings of obedience, and so backfire. *(4)* In making requests of particular people (such as sending them to Peru) the superior will sense whether this particular person can bear the weight of the request or not, for he will be aware of the potential damage to his own authority which would be caused by its irresponsible use. Such an understanding of obedience is therefore self-correcting, for the superior will only ask things that the brother or sister is capable of. Everything should be such, says St Benedict, that 'the strong have something to strive after, while the weak are not discouraged'.[44] *(5)* We have learned many lessons from the mistakes of the past. In earlier centuries these questions were not, either in monasticism or in the secular Church, so self-consciously reflected on and schematically analysed as is now the case. With modern hindsight it is becoming possible to identify principles much more thoroughly, and they have in a new way been *named*, and inscribed on people's consciousness. This makes the concept of the 'abba' that much more difficult to corrupt. *(6)* In extreme circumstances there are ways of replacing abbots.

All that we have been saying is, or should be, applicable to the Church as a whole. Bishops cannot so simply send clergy to Peru, and even less can a vicar send the churchwarden. There is a difference in degree between obedience in a religious community and that in the secular Church, but its nature is the same. It cannot simply be concerned with chains of command such as operate in the army or a big company. It is a way of relating, born of the bonds found in Christian community, and its primary concern is not with jobs to be done, but with persons as individuals and in relationship.

It is only when Christians are well grounded in such an understanding of obedience as this that we can then go on to speak of 'obeying orders', 'obeying superiors'. In the normal run of things all that we have described is elided into request and positive response. It would be nonsense to require an in-depth discussion each time the monastery cow needed milking or the car needed to go to the garage. It would be impossible for the bishop to carry on long sensitive discussions each time he had to give a ruling on something. Obedience can therefore often *look* just like civil or military obedience, but there is a fundamental internal difference in the attitudes of those involved. They are coming at it from a different place.

There are in addition occasions when it can take an even stronger form, but then it is only out of sheer necessity, after all other possibilities have been tried. So the ARCIC final report is able to say: 'Since the bishop has general oversight of the community, he can require the compliance necessary to maintain faith and charity in its daily life. He does not, however, act alone. All those who exercise ministerial authority must recognize their mutual responsibility and interdependence.'[45]

This possibility reveals something unique in the position of the Christian shepherd. We have seen that while his words and acts are formed by the community, and he is midwife to their concretization, they are nevertheless transformed in passing through his hands. His role is quasi-sacramental, and bears with it a particular authority. Bishops, priests and deacons, according to the nature of their respective offices, speak and act with authority. As Christ gave authority to his apostles, so these receive authority at their ordination. This presents problems in a society which believes notionally in equality (even if it is very far from practising it). The main problem is at the psychological level, where many of us have a deep resistance to any notions of authority, superiority or being in some way 'different'. We find, therefore, that some clergy are very keen to play down any apparent differences between themselves and other people. 'I am not any different from you' is acted out day by day in many ministerial lives.

The roots of this lie very far down, partly in a deep, secret anger at terrible abuse of clerical 'power' in the past, as well as painful experience at the hands of priests displaying insensitivity or ostrich-like behaviour. It is also a natural response to society's habit of expecting clergy to fit a stereotyped pattern which is a caricature: many clergy are haunted by the spectre of the stage vicar. However, a problem is not solved by producing a photographic negative of it.

This very desire to be 'the same' as everybody else is also another manifestation of the contemporary cult of individualism. 'I don't want to be different from anybody else' is, first of all, another way of saying, 'I don't want to claim any privileges for myself'. It assumes that to be 'different' is to possess something for yourself that other people don't have. It is like saying, 'I don't want a Rolls-Royce because it would make me different from ordinary people.' Only in a chronically individualistic society could such an attitude be taken towards special roles in the Church. We have lost the equipment to see that the prime reality is the texture of the community, rather than things that each individual 'possesses'. It is to do with the weft and warp of the fabric of the Church, reflecting exactly the unity-in-diversity of the Holy Trinity, where one love circulates between three persons who are equal and the same, and yet each has a particular role in a diversified structure, of which the Father is the root.

Mistaken preoccupation with status is exacerbated by very odd talk current in the Church at the moment, reflected in interest in 'career structures' and 'promotion'. It is possible to imagine a rich, ironic epistle that Paul could have written in response to such talk. Status seems to be in, and yet 'being different' is out. And so we have a decline of the pastoral structures of the family, replaced by a growing vision of the career structures of an institution. Individual advancement can thus sometimes seem to become a higher good than responding to the needs of the Body.

In addition to concepts of possession, status and career, our problem also has to do with assumptions about personhood. Because we presuppose that inside each one of us there is an essential 'me' waiting to get out, we are preoccupied with preserving and protecting this essential me. There is fear that the 'essential me' will be distorted through being pressed into a mould. We feel the 'essential me' needs to be as free as a butterfly, while roles like priesthood lop pieces off it and chain it to a stone wall.

97

Wittgenstein on the other hand faces us with the possibility that the essential 'me' is not there until it has been enabled to come to birth through commerce within the community, with other people. I do not know what the essential me is like until I have it tested and challenged at the external level of relationships-in-community, and this carries with it the unavoidable truth that I will be called upon to fulfil certain roles in society, whatever my walk of life, and these roles will mould me to their shape. Or, rather, they will call themselves forth from me, if such is my potential.

Let us take the example of a young man recently ordained to the priesthood (I take this very male example because the stereotypes we are reacting against here are inevitably associated with men). This priest may be anxious to remain his 'real self', and not to become some clerical stereotype. However, the person he is at the moment, although he may be very happy with it, may not be the person he is destined to be. That can only be discovered by commerce with something outside himself. If he is truly called to be a priest, then there is a whole new way of life to grow into. In the process he is bound to be changed. With luck and God's grace he will grow into that which he was meant to be. He will inevitably become different: both from what he was, and from other people who have not been through that particular experience. Endless visiting, enabling, reconciling, presiding at worship, praying, studying, reflecting, inevitably make you different from people who do not do the same things in the same proportion. After a while there is a sense in which you will not recognize yourself. This is because the Old Man is passing away, in order to become the New Man, to which you have been destined.

This change can be perceived as a bad thing if we think it stops at the individual. But in the economy of the Church, when one person is changed the whole Body is changed. The distinctiveness of the priest only becomes a problem if the priest is seen as an individual. When we see his 'differentness' as the possession of the whole Body of Christ, the problem fades away.

The 'difference', as St Paul rightly says, is concerned with the building up of the structure of the body. Not all can be hands, not all can be left ears. Each part has its function. That 'something different' which is found in a priest does not separate him from people: it simply makes him a distinctive ingredient in the glue which holds the Body together.

Looking at this from another angle, it is possible to see that in a society in which the bonds between people are so superficial, individuals will naturally be reluctant to become 'different', for this can destroy the last shreds that remain of any sense of corporateness. To be different is to stand apart, and the clerical life can be a very lonely one. Giving a high profile to the clerical role can feel like a denial of solidarity. But this should not be so in the Church, where the whole enterprise of relating to each other is conducted at the level of a 'practice'. Apartness then becomes an ingredient in the process towards that higher unity which is a sign of the Kingdom. That has never worked out through a bland equality of ingredients, but through the very strength of their differentness. It is just the same in cooking.

The truth of the matter is that those who are ordained into holy orders are entering into a Tradition, the Tradition of the Christian ministry of bishops, priests and deacons. As we have found, such a process involves an apprenticeship during which the person is changed, becoming someone they could not have foreseen beforehand, but whom they were destined to be: their real selves.

Only by having the courage to lose themselves in order to find themselves can Christians build up the Church. It applies to all, whatever the vocation, because we all exercise responsibility and leadership in different ways. There are times when a member of the PCC is spiritual father to the priest, and indeed in any meeting, different people will at certain moments be mother, guide and midwife to the community's search for the will of God. At such moments such persons will often need the courage to be 'different'. Whether layfolk, bishops, priests, deacons or other ministers, only when we have been prepared to lose ourselves in order to find ourselves can we dare to be spiritual fathers-and-mothers within the Body of Christ.

Jesus showed what we have to do with what we regard as our very self. He laid it down. To be dead is to be very different indeed. To be the risen Lord is to burst all the bounds of sameness. Yet he, through the difference to end all differences, has become the mother and father of us all, and is closer to us than anyone else can be; through his 'difference' we are one with the Father. *'Vive la différence.'*

Depth psychology has established beyond doubt how important it is for us to be in touch with our own past childhood. Any quest to know ourselves better and to find healing for old wounds lies in a journey backwards through our history. Such a journey can often give moments of startling revelation, as some event or relationship in our earlier years becomes the explanation of why we are as we are. So we can see why a difficult relationship with our father may have made us resentful of authority-figures, or some mistaken mother's idea of what was good for baby has left him with a particular obsession. The journey back to these roots is a journey of self-discovery, and as such is a path to healing.

This is as true of communities and of institutions as it is of individuals. It is a legitimate thing to ask therefore whether the Church is in touch with its past. If not, in which areas, and to what extent does this impair its attempts to be the Church today? These questions are especially relevant to the Church of England, although they are also important for all Churches without exception.

The Anglican Church needs to understand better its relationship to the past in order that it may attain a better understanding of itself, and in order to recognize things in itself which it does not recognize. This process is happening at this time to whole nations in the Soviet Union; it happened in the German Protestant Churches immediately after the War; and someday, we may hope, it will happen in South Africa. In all these situations outsiders see many intangible things which insiders cannot see because they are too much part of them. Part of the disentanglement process has to be a journey into the past.

For us in the Anglican Church this means embracing much more wholeheartedly a breathtaking panorama of things sometimes referred to as the Great Church, that reality of the Body of Christ beside which Anglicanism is dwarfed: from the Church of the Apostles it branches out to the ancient churches of Syria and the

Near East, and the vast riches to which they gave birth over the centuries; thence we move across to the great phenomenon of the Byzantine Church, whose immeasurable depths were tributary to the formation of our own ancestors. On we go, wheeling round to the manifold traditions of the West, and the accumulation of wisdom, mistakes, wrong turnings, bursts of inspiration and painful wounds which have all contributed to our habits of thought, our ideals and our phobias and taboos. They have all given us things which we cannot recognize in ourselves. Rising out of the midst of that manifoldness looms finally a great form which becomes unavoidable, in whichever direction we may look, the inheritance and the reality of Rome. Then comes that rude awakening, the Reformation, whose various member Churches are all custodians of debris of a fragmented tradition, and all of whom must be part of and contributory to the final healing, whatever form it will take. All of this has stamped us with our fingerprints, provided us with our prejudices and presuppositions, and left us with wounds, fears and distortions which can only be healed by owning and recognizing all that has gone before. We cannot know ourselves until we have travelled back through it all.

For Anglicans the heart of the matter is Rome. Our Church is Roman in its organization, its thought and its liturgy. It is an indisputable product of Rome, a variant on a Roman theme, both directly through all it has retained, and indirectly through its Reformation inheritance. For the Anglican Church to believe it has any ecclesial reality apart from Rome is genetically impossible. Here we have touched a highly neuralgic point which makes us excruciatingly pained ('Aha!', says the psychologist; 'we are getting down to business').

What are Anglicans to make of Rome? We have few illusions about its problems and failings, not least its temptation to think in terms of power and centralism rather than service and listening, problems not helped by a current occupant of the papal office who does not, if we may speak the truth in love, seem fully to have grasped either the difference between Tradition and traditionalism, nor that between spiritual fatherhood and paternalism. Nevertheless, the Great Church, which includes the Orthodox, the Protestants and all the main Churches of the Christian Tradition, demands our attention, and for us Rome in this is an essential reference-point. Indeed, the see of Peter is so much our inheritance that we should not allow Romans to have it all to themselves. Even if it will be a very long time before reunion is possible, Anglicans have unique gifts to bring to bear in prophesying to Rome on what may be the vocation of the papacy. We may have to suffer remaining on the outside for longer yet, but that does not prevent us taking a burning and persistent interest, and speaking our mind in the process. Despite all Rome's drawbacks as at present constituted, it is such a primeval archetype in our psychological make-up that any rediscovery of who we are cannot hope to get anywhere by dodging it.

There are perhaps two ways in which it commands our attention. First, there is the vast, deep-rooted Tradition of the Western Church as a whole. Here is a cruse of wisdom and folly on the grandest of scales, and with a guts and readiness to acknowledge the dark physicality and bile of human nature, and the outrageous grandeur of our destiny, that cannot easily be found among polite Anglo-Saxons when left to themselves. Anglicanism's great merits bring with them the fault of an incapacity for the large-scale and audacious, and no great inclination to strive beyond homely horizons. Its gifts of comprehensiveness and understatement are never likely to set the world alight unless they rediscover the deep mulch and vigour of the Tradition of the Western Church, whose whole history is part of our psyche, a doorway to our very selves, if we would acknowledge it. This history, particularly from the time of the Church's re-launch under Charlemagne, is intimately part and parcel of the birth of modern Western culture, and to ignore it or keep it at a distance is to hide from our own unconscious. It is a woeful lot for any people or any Church to think that history is not vital.

This Tradition is dominated by Rome. For all its faults and limitations, it has a largeness about it which enables much more audacious creativity than is possible among Anglicans, where there is a profound inability to adapt to other cultures, and a deadly, endemic propensity to get stuck. All of this so far is simply an outline of the grandeur of the Tradition of the Great Church, stretching from the shores of the Mediterranean to the frozen north, and which eventually coalesced around Byzantium and Rome. Our 'feel' for it is too faint.

The second matter to command our attention is the city of Rome and its bishop. Even to mention any thought of accepting the

Pope's spiritual fatherhood once again (apart from any negotiations safely taking place in the ecclesiastical stratosphere) is still to many English people like touching a bare nerve in a tooth. We wince, we shudder, we tar people who mention such a thing with a brush which makes them beyond serious consideration. Here is a great wound, preserved by the toughness of tradition. It is such a deep psychological gash that we shall never be whole until its healing is complete. It is difficult to know how that may happen, given the real faults of both sides, but until it does we are denied a whole dimension which makes for ecclesial life and vitality, the completion of the structure of spiritual fatherhood.

Here we come up against the equivocal nature of the world-wide Anglican Communion. The good reason for its cultivation is the perception that we are set in one world, and need to pursue with absolute commitment the contacts we have beyond the bounds of the British Isles. The Third World in particular needs us and we need it far more than we think.

The problem is that the way we go about it is far too narrow. It is shown up with terrible and embarrassing clarity by the Anglican cycle of intercession used in so many of our churches. How can we pray in great detail for Anglicans in Tanzania or Canada as if Methodists, Roman Catholics and Lutherans did not exist there? And how can we with any sense of reality trip so lightly over countries like Vietnam, France and Czechoslovakia? It all follows too closely and painfully the contours of a faded British Empire, and carries with it the stunted, almost incestuous feel of a world turned in upon its own limited horizons. In striving to look beyond the bounds of our little island, we have only succeeded in stranding ourselves on a bigger island, the *petit monde* of Anglicanism. This little world is in too many ways plagued with stuckness, introversion, and the hardened arteries of Wippeldom, to succeed in being *microcosm*.

One glaring example of this is seen in places in Southern Africa, where Anglicans conspicuously fail to do anything about inculturation of the liturgy, being beaten hands down by the Roman Catholics, who, for all their problems, manifest a freedom and openness that can only be found among bodies which are sure of their tradition. We have exported establishment stuffiness and are intent on keeping it alive, in the teeth of the vibrant reality of the Church Catholic. In many if not most parts of the Anglican

Communion local relationships with other denominations are becoming a greater reality than the connection with Canterbury, most conspicuously among the layfolk. Yet there is an increasing tendency to see the Anglican Church as an *-ism*, a parallel Church, sufficient unto itself and competent in all ecclesial respects. If this concept of a free-standing 'ecclesia' follows its due course, it would eventually become logical to speak of Anglican sacraments, and an Anglican Bible, and that would be heresy. It is the religion of the beer-making kit. Haunting the British Church by law established is a far-too-British ghost of Empire, and a questionable sense of effortless superiority. Anglicans in other parts of the world may be too tempted to play up to that, or, as is often the case, sit lightly to it yet fail to see the limitations of the cramped English religious culture which they perpetuate.

The riches of the Anglican inheritance wait for their fulfilment in the whole Body of Christ. In a setting which is purely Anglican they have run their course, and are now threatened with exhaustion. So, for instance, comprehensiveness now seems to distinguish us from Protestants, Orthodox and Roman Catholics by having come to mean a sidestepping of the claims of God, an inability to live in terms of his sovereignty. Anything goes, in a Church where sovereignty has been transferred to human reason and the values of the twentieth-century West. The fulfilment of our truly proud inheritance can only come beyond itself. It cannot come by turning the seventeenth-century divines, comprehensiveness and the 'Anglican genius' into demi-gods. I myself am proud of those things, as part of my history and the genius of the Church in which I was born. But I do wish they could be set in the greater context of the whole Church, where they will no longer have to bear more weight than they can carry.

When we turn to that essential 'kit' of paraphernalia, rigmaroles and 'card games' which are the stuff of spiritual and ecclesial life, we find the Anglican cupboard to be very bare. The passing of the Book of Common Prayer has revealed how much was invested in that alone. For the common people it was only for a little while enough to hold them, but now that it has gone, we see how slender were the threads which held our life together in a common ecclesial identity. We seem to have ended up in a land without landmarks.

The Anglican salon needs to unbrick the doorways through to the rest of the house. It needs all the Churches now, not tomorrow, and all the Churches need that mysterious chemistry of orientation which somehow has to do with Rome. The current papacy and Vatican need to be called to reform: they need the Anglican genius. But the need is mutual.

There are some in Anglicanism who already see things in this kind of way. It is not very helpful to speak in terms of parties, but while there are people from a variety of positions who would be sympathetic to such a picture as that just given, many sympathizers would be found amongst what is sometimes called the 'Catholic wing', and there we find for various reasons considerable disarray. As this disarray has consequences for the whole Church it would be good to identify some of the possible causes, in the quest for renewal. The members of this constituency would never again, we hope, seek renewal in the hope of reviving party rivalries, but rather the role of a leaven for the lump.

The first problem which is clearly identifiable here is a debilitating weakness in the field of learning, and the proper appreciation of the fruits of scholarly study, and imaginative reflection upon them. There is too little hard thinking going on. As a result, there is among many a tremendous sense of being stuck, and not knowing where to move. Old certainties are then held onto without being backed up by serious thinking.

Second, there is a resulting narrowness in the vision of what constitutes the Catholic Tradition. By being narrow it fails to be Catholic. The diversity-in-unity of, say, the Roman Catholic Church in Europe or in South America is light years away from this rather tightly drawn world. A good example of this is seen in the approach to worship: many so-called Anglo-Catholics treat the liturgical provisions of Vatican II as a static model, to be implemented more or less according to the letter. The trouble is that amongst Roman Catholics, as any participation in international Roman Catholic life brings home, the liturgy is dynamic. It is part of an ongoing debate in which all participate (even if with varying degrees of frustration). It is changing and developing as it goes along. And there is debate in the press, in articles, conferences and so on. We are cut off from that. We can receive little from it, and can contribute nothing. But if we try to produce a text-book copy of the 'norm', we end up with something very different. It can be like the 'English' ways maintained by aged expatriates in Caracas or Alicante. All certainly English, but nothing like real life at home.

We are not part of the debate. We are out of the circuit. We are inevitably doing something different.

One urgent need, therefore, is for travel. In today's world anyone who believes in the catholicity of the Church should travel, if free to do so. They should learn languages, make contacts and friends, get in on the debate. No group can seriously call itself 'Catholic' today if it fails to do so. If I were to speak about the catholicity of the Church, then I would need to put my feet where my mouth is. Those who might be called Anglo-Catholics need to make sure that they are not odd, insular and provincial before making great claims about being 'catholic'. This can only be ascertained by travel in which real and lasting contacts are made. It demands more than mere window-shopping: it needs bridge-building, if for no other reason than this, that participating in worship with people of another country repeatedly brings home with a shock the realization that God isn't an Englishman (using the word advisedly). Some people will object: 'We haven't the languages, the contacts or the money.' Here is a task for those societies which aim to stand for the Tradition in the Church of England, as well as for the missionary societies. With their centralized resources these problems could be overcome: contacts made, money raised, and timid adventurers encouraged. There is no excuse in the modern world for this all-too-English constituency to stay as provincial as it is.

Third, many avowed Catholics in the Church of England have a perception of the Church which is desperately narrow and historically superficial. How many know what the *Hadrianum* is?[46] How can they hope to understand what is meant by *Romanitas* if they do not? How many have anything but a passing acquaintance with Orthodoxy, or any of the other Eastern Churches? It is difficult to claim catholicity in a situation of such ignorance in today's world. That is universally acknowledged today, for instance, in the field of liturgy. We cannot understand our liturgy without being familiar with the Eastern inheritance.

Nothing is to be gained, either, by being selective. Lutherans and Methodists are custodians of debris of the Tradition which we need for our souls' health, and they need us for theirs (no small consideration!).

Fourth, Catholic Anglicans' view of catholicity can be superficial in an important regard, and this is tragically displayed in their lack of unity. They have failed to see that to fight for ideals *against* the establishment can only be effective to a degree, and after that it begins to corrupt. Catholic Christians need to be loyal and obedient to their chief shepherds in all things reasonable and lawful, and also listen with greater generosity to others within the Church with whom they disagree. There has not been that commerce within the *koinonia* of the Church, whose characteristic is listening and obedience amongst all, and with the chief shepherds of the flock, which is the very stuff of healthy life in the Church, and far more important than most victories gained for this external practice and that point of doctrine. It is tempting but fatal to batten on to packages whose details are so sacrosanct that they become something to beat other people around the head with. Flag-waving is always fun, but throws a big shadow behind it. In concentrating on externals and particular forms of devotion as banners, Catholic Anglicans have neglected the more demanding spiritual heritage of the Tradition, perhaps particularly with regard to obedience. I will give another liturgical example. In the Archdiocese of Milan parishes are only allowed to celebrate the Ambrosian Mass. They could not use the Roman Mass without the Archbishop's permission, and if requested, that would most likely be refused. Anglican parishes which use the Roman Missal without their Bishop's leave may therefore like to reflect on whether the unity of that part of the Ecclesia in which they are rooted may not be more benefited if Roman standards of obedience are given a higher priority than Roman external observances.

A warning is needed here. Once again we find ourselves in the situation of the juggler, with many skittles to keep in the air. The Church of England being what it is, care has to be taken that obedience is not confused with becoming 'establishment poodles' (a serious warning for religious communities there, too). The road winds precariously between the two dangers of being 'yes-men' and being 'no-men'. There is a raised place in the middle in which is found that sacramental commerce within the Body which we have identified as a 'practice', something to be pursued because it is very, very good, something which is an 'internal good' higher than any 'external fruits'. If that leads to a rediscovery of the sacramental *koinonia* of the Church, then that must surely put an end to any further talk of parties and factions. There are plenty of battles to be fought, but they are rarely worth such symbols of division.

· In the meantime either we accept living with the essential structures of the Church of England as they are, or we transfer to another of the mainstream Churches. That is the only *obedient* way, and if we have faith that the long-term destiny of Christians is to converge, we shall know that the anguish of such situations will be led eventually towards a resolution, in the Lord's good time.

As we have seen, an essential characteristic of the spiritual father is that he should be obedient—his own obedience makes for obedience (the 'listening' out of which unity is built) in the community. 'Anglo-Catholics' have unfortunately often gone more for the external goods than the internal. Obedience is a fruit in itself which is worth any number of those things. We may need to sacrifice many secondary goods for that primary good which is the living-out of obedience—that is, listening with the whole of ourselves. 'My sheep are the ones which hear my voice.' Being obedient ourselves, we will be in a much better position to call a whole Church to obedience. Obedience builds unity. Lack of unity is fatal among such a small constituency in such a small Church, and banners alone are not enough to produce it.

All Anglicans who prize the Great Tradition have plenty to make them of good cheer, if only they would recognize how rich is our inheritance. The Anglican Church is blessed with great gifts, not least in pastoral wisdom, and personal and corporate holiness. The threads are all there, waiting to be pulled together by a renewed vision which will bring the Tradition to a fresh interpretation and a new enfleshing for our time, free from flag-waving and party spirit, and zealous for the unity of all.

There are too many parties and points of view, all standing their ground, all disobedient. No one can claim a monopoly on the Momentum of the Church, not even the Pope. The Holy Spirit is impossible to grasp: he calls us to be divine jugglers. He flits to and fro amongst the hurly-burly of the Church; here and there we may sight him. The history of the Church is his wake, the future is wherever he may blow. He wheels and circles with never-exhausted life, yet is so deep and strong as to roll us forward in his eternal current. His Momentum is ours too. It is our Mother and our Father, it is our daughter and our son. We create and are created as the Kingdom unfolds. In this *microcosm* we stand in worship before the glory of God, in the same moment helping Christ distribute his bread in market-place and kitchen, and receiving bread in return.

The Great Church is, for all Christians, the hidden ancestor of all that makes us what we are. She lives today, carrying us as she carried the apostles beyond their known horizons. It is time to go with her, so that she may show us that all is bigger than we thought.

# CHAPTER 11 *Beyond our Horizons*

And so we come to where we started. Brother Leo, the former Marcus, sits in the shade of a tree waiting for the other monks to arrive. It is three years to the day since he gained entrance, by sheer dint of perseverance. What was it that drove him here? He can no longer remember clearly. Of one thing he is quite sure, however. The reality is utterly different from the descriptions in rules or books. 'I see now', he thinks, 'why Father Benedict said that the gospel can only be lived, not described.' He remembers trying to keep a straight face when the old man had said in all seriousness: 'You meet the Lord in the liturgy, in the brethren, in the guests, in the pots and pans, and in the cows.' He thinks of the old bishop he has left. He too understands these things, without being a monk.

Other brethren drift up, and soon most of them are there, taking advantage of the cool shade of late afternoon at the zenith of summer. It is too hot to hold their conference indoors.

The old abbot gives a long discourse on the troubles of the times. He is in sombre mood. 'I know you think all is well with the world, but appearances deceive. We only see very little. Never mistake the part for the whole.'

Eventually he comes round to talking of his new version of the Rule, and how he had had to adapt the Tradition of the ancients to our lukewarm age. 'It is only a *little* rule,' he says, 'a *preparation* for entering on the gospel way. Never mistake the part for the whole. The whole is always bigger than that which we can see, and even bigger than all we aspire after. In our tepid age many things are diluted and fragmented. We must set our feet in the large room of the holy Tradition, where we shall find life. And let us pursue the will of God in holy obedience, for there we find our unity with Christ. He is calling us to be good stewards who will pass on the priceless treasure of the gospel to the Church which is to come. Our world is worse than lukewarm. We have to prepare while we still have the chance. Now as never before is there a need for wise men and women who build their house on a rock. Now as never before is there a need for watchmen on the walls of Christendom. Like the good watchman let us watch, and announce what we see.'

The warmth and the sun seem to belie all he says. The crickets lull the hearers, all is peace and repose.

Yet St Benedict knows it is time to disregard such a comforting scene and prepare for the winter. 'I may be wrong, but I feel that the temper of the present times will lead to nothing but darkness. "Now is the hour for us to rise from sleep." Let us then be awake and watchful, with our lamps burning, prepared for the coming of a night which may be very great.'

The unexpected words reduce everyone to silence. Even the crickets are still for a moment. Brother Leo feels the weight of some awesome imperative. Something of daunting importance seems to have been placed on their shoulders, which could affect the destiny of many. He has always been overawed by Father Benedict, but particularly when he speaks like this. The silence goes on and on.

Suddenly it is broken by a piercing howl in their midst. The cook has turned his gaze over the low wall, and now stands electrified. All rise to look over the wall, and stare in horror. The three monastic donkeys have found their way into the vegetable patch. While the community was otherwise distracted they have been feeding at leisure. In a subsistence economy this is no joke. Some brethren rush off, suddenly stop and rush back, to bow and ask leave. Those who are concerned about the old precept that a monk never rushes try to walk fast while making it look leisurely: the newest forget themselves and rush down the hillside like barbarians. Surrounded by shouting, gesticulating and pushing humans, the donkeys stand like the only true monks in the place, indifferent, unbudging, serene.

The father of the community struggles down the stony slope on Brother Leo's arm. 'I always find it difficult to talk about such things, Brother Leo. They need to be said, but we can end up almost thinking we are important. Thanks be to God, that he has sent us three angels to save us from that. The Church should not be so earnest, Leo. Earnestness is a sure sign that Christ has not yet succeeded in making us whole.'

The brethren have managed to get the beasts away from doing any more damage to the cook's prize broccoli, but the donkeys are in stubborn mood. 'Yes, the wholeness of Christ', muses St Benedict, grunting slightly as he goes. 'Christians see many things as being so serious, so important, which indeed they are. But that's a very dangerous mood to be in. High ideals always mask an undergrowth of folly and sin; *always*, dear Brother Leo. How ridiculous to see ourselves as serious or important.'

He is getting out of breath and stops. 'The Church is a stage, dear Brother. What is acted out there is much more than mere seriousness or importance. It is, Brother Leo, would that we recognized it, an excruciating tragi-comedy. But of a breathtaking greatness. If only we, the Church, would watch that drama.'

# NOTES

1 Rule of St Benedict, chapter 73.
2 Jean O'Rourke, in *The Tablet*, 21 January 1989, p. 68.
3 *Faith in the City*. Church House Publishing, 1985.
4 G. Guiver, *Company of Voices* (SPCK 1988), p. 35.
5 Fergus Kerr, *Theology after Wittgenstein*. Blackwell 1986. For an introduction to the many ways in which Wittgenstein is interpreted, see J. Mark, 'Wittgenstein, Theology and Wordless Faith'. *New Blackfriars*, October 1989, pp. 423–43.
6 *Confessions*, Book 1, chapter 6.
7 *Culture and Value*, ed. G. H. von Wright and H. Nyman, trans. P. Winch (Oxford 1980), p. 11; quoted in Kerr, p. 189.
8 ibid., p. 65.
9 *Wittgenstein's Lectures Cambridge 1932–1935*, ed. A. Ambrose (Oxford 1979), p. 78; quoted in Kerr, p. 77.
10 ibid., p. 115.
11 ibid., p. 115.
12 *On Certainty*, ed. G. E. M. Anscombe and G. H. von Wright, trans. D. Paul and G. E. M. Anscombe (Oxford 1969), para. 148; quoted in Kerr, p. 101.
13 ibid., p. 140.
14 ibid., p. 55.
15 *Zettel*, ed. G. E. M. Anscombe and G. H. von Wright, trans. G. E. M. Anscombe (Oxford 1967), para. 382; quoted in Kerr, p. 49.
16 I prefer this to the usual translation: 'forms of life', which is more likely to mislead here.
17 Kerr, p. 188.
18 Psalm 80.10ff.
19 John 15.1.
20 T. S. Eliot, *Four Quartets*.
21 ibid.
22 See J. E. Vaux, *Church Folk Lore* (2nd edn 1902), and other works cited in *Company of Voices* (see n. 4), p. 273.
23 F. Kline, *The instruments of creative discipline in spiritual and cultural traditions* (Cistercian Studies XXIV, 1989, No. 3), p. 227.
24 *Company of Voices*, chapter 1.
25 Alasdair MacIntyre, *After Virtue*. Duckworth 1981.
26 ibid., p. 11.
27 ibid., pp. 1ff.

28 ACCM Occasional Paper No. 29, May 1988.
29 *Company of Voices*, pp. 177ff.
30 Psalm 106.15.
31 See note 5.
32 ibid., p. 76.
33 1 Peter 2.5 and Psalm 102.14.
34 Kerr, p. 45.
35 Ruth Benedict, *Patterns of Culture* (first pub. 1935; Routledge reprint 1961), pp. 15ff.
36 *Ep.* 64.11 (PL 77, col. 1187), quoted in A. Chupungco, *Cultural Adaptation of the Liturgy* (New York 1982), p. 26.
37 MacIntyre, pp. 175ff.
38 ibid., p. 177.
39 See, for example, *Company of Voices* (see n. 4) pp. 84–91.
40 ARCIC—*The Final Report* (CTS/SPCK 1981), pp. 33 and 53–5.
41 *Ep.* 52.7.
42 Reproduced by permission of the Sisters of the Love of God, Fairacres.
43 Translation by J. McCann, 1970.
44 RSB 64.
45 ARCIC, p. 54.
46 This was the liturgical book which Pope Hadrian sent to Charlemagne for performance of the Roman liturgy. It was hopelessly incomplete, and had to be supplemented by material from Gallic sources. This hybrid was the ancestor of the Roman liturgy that we know, and is as important to the story of 'Roman-ness' as 1066 or Magna Carta are to Britishness.

# INDEX